ZDRAVKO STEFANOVIC

Cover design by Gerald Lee Monks
Cover design resources from iStockPhoto.com | LifeJourneys | Soldier
iStockPhoto.com | D-Keine | Bible
Inside design by Aaron Troia

The author assumes full responsibility for the accuracy of all facts and quotations as cited in this book.

You can obtain additional copies of this book by calling toll-free 1-800-765-6955 or by visiting AdventistBookCenter.com.

Library of Congress Cataloging-in-Publication Data
Names: Stefanovic, Zdravko, author.
Title: Unforsaken : the story of Milan / Zdravko Stefanovic.
Description: Nampa, Idaho : Pacific Press Publishing Association, [2021] | Includes bibliographical references. | Summary: "The inspiring story of Milan's conversion and faith journey in the midst of a wartorn country"— Provided by publisher.
Identifiers: LCCN 2021016386 | ISBN 9780816367634 | ISBN 9780816367641 (ebook)
Subjects: LCSH: Milan (Christian) | Christian biography—Bosnia and Herzegovina.
Classification: LCC BR1725.M443 S74 2021 | DDC 286.7092 [B]—dc23
LC record available at https://lccn.loc.gov/2021016386

June 2021

CONTENTS

INTRODUCTION

The power of God is more displayed in the [process of true conversion], than in the creation of heaven and earth: for at the creation no power opposed; but at the conversion of [one person], devil and hell, and even fellow-creatures, are opposed.

—Joseph Wolff (1795–1862)

This book is based on a true story that began on the brink of the Second World War, though the names of the characters have been changed. The story is about a man named Milan whose faith in God led him step-by-step from despair to hope when he needed it most. His life demonstrated that he had found forgiveness, purpose, and joy in his Savior's loving arms. Moreover, he firmly believed that his prayers on behalf of others, including his family members, were heard by God. In fact, those who knew him best recognized his contagious zeal for spiritual matters. The greatest privilege of my life was to grow up in his family, with parents who lived out their conviction that knowing God is our most treasured possession and that He is the source of our hope and blessings.

My father spent a lot of time not just reading the passages from the Bible but truly "feasting" on them. He readily admitted that his life depended on the lessons found in the sacred pages. Moreover, my father was eager to share those precious lessons with everyone around him. In our daily family worships, the Psalms were read aloud more frequently than any other part of Scripture. This is because the Psalms present the complete human experience, ranging from fear to trust, from sadness to joy, and from folly to wisdom. This attitude of love toward the sacred passages made a lasting impression on how I read the Bible even today. As you read, I invite you to allow my father's story to touch your heart. May his faithful example help you grow in your walk with our Savior.

The setting of Milan's story is a tiny country in southeastern Europe known as Bosnia. Around thirteen centuries ago, Slavic people moved into the central region of the Balkan Peninsula—an area that is notorious for its tumultuous history. As powerful armies from east and west passed through the region and new rulers exercised their control, the social and cultural landscapes continuously changed. On a few occasions in the second half of the fourteenth century, the local rulers were able to gain autonomy or near autonomy, leading to a period of independence. Since then, Bosnia has been a part of the Ottoman Empire; the Austro-Hungarian Empire; the Kingdom of Serbs, Croats, and Slovenes; modern Yugoslavia; and finally, the independent Bosnia and Herzegovina.

At the beginning of the twentieth century, the first Adventist pastors began their ministry in the capital city of Sarajevo following the work of a few pioneer colporteurs. This window of opportunity was opened thanks to the constitution introduced under Austrian rule. It contained some very generous provisions regarding religion. For example, Roman Catholics, Orthodox Christians, Jews, and Muslims could worship on any day of the week. Unfortunately, these good times did not last very long; atrocities such as ethnic cleansings committed during conflicts and wars illustrate this fact. One would expect that organized religions would point human beings toward the ways of love, peace, and multiculturalism. Unfortunately, this simply was not the case. In fact, very often, people who tried to live up to the ideals of their faith did so at great risk of losing their property and lives. Milan's story is a witness of such a strong faith.

CHAPTER ONE

A DIFFICULT CHILDHOOD

You are my hiding place;
you will protect me from trouble
and surround me with songs of deliverance.

I will instruct you and teach you in the way you should go;
I will counsel you with my loving eye on you.
—Psalm 32:7, 8

Milan's story begins almost a century ago in the little town of Derventa in northern Bosnia. Here, the brick buildings and farmlands nestle against the green hills near the Ukrina River.

Home

In a humble two-room cottage, Milan cooked a simple meal. He was dressed in nothing more than a long shirt whose tattered hem came to his knees, and his calloused feet were bare, as always, on the rough wooden floor. From a cot at the far side of the room, Milan's two younger sisters peered hungrily through the smoke from the woodstove at the frying pan. The stovepipe had broken earlier in the year, and it had stayed that way. The door of the house stood open to let in light and let out the smoke.

Suddenly, through the open door, a shriek pierced the silence. "What's this, Milan? What are you doing by the stove?" A tired, middle-aged woman entered unsteadily. Her dress was stained, and her eyes were glazed and bloodshot. Milan said nothing, and the girls began to whimper.

"Be quiet!" the woman snapped at them. "My head is splitting. Can't I have a little peace in my own home?"

She staggered over to the stove for a look at the food. "Oh my, what a feast. Eggs and potatoes and real butter! Where did you get all of this?" she demanded, turning on her son with a glare.

"From the store," Milan answered softly with downcast eyes. "Aunty gave them to me after I helped out this morning."

"And you couldn't wait until I returned, you greedy boy? Don't you know I could have traded the eggs for some plum brandy at the corner shop? Let this teach you a lesson!" She raised her hand to strike, but Milan darted around her and dashed for the door. Stopping on the threshold, he turned and looked at his mother beseechingly. The girls were crying.

"Mother, please. Why don't you lie down and sleep it off?"

"How dare you?" she cried. "First, you shame me in front of our relatives by accepting charity, and now you shame me in front of my own daughters by implying that I am drunk."

"No, Mother, that isn't what—"

"Be quiet! Who do you think you are to talk back to me like that? Maybe this will close your mouth." And with that, she grabbed the frying pan and hurled it at Milan's head, spilling the precious food and wasting the reward of his hard work. Barely dodging the heavy pan, Milan turned and fled. Curses followed him down the street while neighbors watched and shook their heads.

Later that evening, Milan crawled back home from the nearby cemetery where he hid among the crumbling tombstones when his mother was in an alcoholic fit. She was asleep and snoring in the back room when he snuck in. The girls were still awake from hunger and fear. He found a hunk of moldy bread and divided it between them—Milan made sure to eat the smallest portion, giving more to his sisters. Then they tried to go to sleep, crowded on the cot, with half-empty stomachs and heavy hearts. Reassured by his presence, the girls gradually fell asleep. But Milan lay there for some time, wondering why his home was a place of fear and abuse instead of the refuge it should be. He felt very much alone. Then, acting on a mysterious impulse that came from somewhere he couldn't define, Milan prayed silently—a plea for help from a lost child. And the Comforter responded in kind, with a divine assurance from above that filled and soothed him in the darkness.

* * * * *

Milan's childhood was difficult, set in an unstable home. His mother, Vida—by nature a mischievous and lighthearted woman who loved to sing and dance to traditional Slavic songs—had been worn down by years of family tragedies, social ostracism, and substance abuse. Her first husband, Stefan, Milan's father, had been killed in a logging accident when she was still a young woman. Her second husband was absent most of the time, serving in the king's army and sending very little money back to the family. And her oldest son, who had been sent to the plains of Vojvodina to learn a trade and become a provider for the family, had snapped and killed himself after being harshly mistreated by a supervisor.

Vida was a stubborn, independent woman who did not fit in with her community's rigid Orthodox or Catholic faiths. She did not attend religious services and was shunned by most of her neighbors as a result. In an act of defiance, Vida turned to fortune-telling to supplement her income. In the patterns made by coffee grounds and thrown beans, she would predict the futures of anxious, doubt-ridden people, assuaging their uncertainties with falsehoods and deceit. But though this supplemented Vida's income, it only served to further distance her from her community.

Without the support of her husband and society, Vida turned to drinking. After, and sometimes before, her long shifts at the textile factory, she would spend her meager earnings on *šljivovica*—the plum brandy that ruined so many lives. And Vida smoked, a habit that was not only deadly to her health but fatal to her social status because in her traditional society, no respectable woman smoked. So instead of caring for her children and facing her problems, Vida chose to drown her sorrow in poison and deny her responsibilities. This was the chaos in which Milan spent his childhood.

Refuge

Children's laughter, as pure and playful as the glistening river, floated up into a summer sky. Half a dozen or so boys played down by the Ukrina, the little river that meandered through farm fields and slid by the town on her way to join her bigger sister, the broad Sava River. The boys were from all faiths and cultures: Orthodox boys, Catholic boys, Muslim boys, and even Roma boys. All were united in their innocent childhood games, splashing and ducking each other in the cool water under the hot sun.

A little distance upstream, Milan waded waist-deep near the riverbank. When the other boys noticed what he was up to, they fell silent and watched. Sure-footed, Milan stepped on the unseen river bottom, careful to avoid slippery rocks and sucking mud. When he reached a spot where the roots of a willow made a little sheltered inlet, Milan carefully stirred up sediment with a branch. Soon the clear waters turned as brown as his sunbaked skin. Milan waited for a few moments, then slowly sank down into the water. His eyes were unfocused, but Milan's hands moved like water snakes with the sluggish current. Suddenly, the water in front of him burst into a froth, and out of the spray, Milan lifted a large, plump trout.

"Hooray!" the boys cheered. "He's done it again! Now we will have fried fish for lunch!"

"Come over here and take him from me!" Milan shouted. "I'm not finished fishing."

In this manner, he caught several more fish—enough to feed the gang and bring home some supper. At least Milan's mother wouldn't be able to find fault with him for this. These fish were given to him by no one. Milan caught them all on his own.

The boys cleaned and cooked the fish over a brushwood fire, sending a black spiral into the blue sky. The aroma made their mouths water and their stomachs growl. Boys always seem to be hungry, but especially so after a spirited river romp. When the meal was ready, they split it into even portions and held the coal-hot food in leaves, blowing on it to cool.

Just as the boys were about to attempt their first scorching mouthfuls, Milan spoke up. "Hey, shouldn't we, you know, say a prayer or something?"

"Why?" asked one of the bigger boys. "Are you a holy man all of a sudden? You don't go to Mass. And isn't your mother into fortune-telling?"

Milan hung his head, his face burning with shame. Why did he have to speak up? What urged him to talk about something he knew nothing about?

"No, he's right," Petar said. "The priest at my church says we should thank God for our blessings."

"Yes," Ivan agreed. "My priest says that we should be grateful to Mary for her daily mercies."

"The imam at my mosque says we should always thank Allah before taking food," chimed in Omer.

"So whom should we pray to?" Milan asked, scratching his head.

"It doesn't matter, as long as we are grateful," replied Rejep, a Roma boy.

They bowed their heads in gratitude for a solemn, silent moment and then devoured the fish. Afterward, with full stomachs, the boys lay in the grass near the riverbank, chattering about silly nothings. Later, when Milan returned home with the fish, his mother was pleased with him, and the girls ate until they were stuffed.

* * * * *

The Ukrina River was a place of refuge and a source of sustenance for Milan. Not only was it a place where he could lose himself in the cool waters, the exhausting games of childhood, and the absorption of fishing, but it was also a place that provided gifts to those who were brave enough to find them. In the spring, when the melting snow swelled the riverbanks, Milan would take his sisters on canoeing expeditions through the verdant halls of blossoming riverbank trees. In the summer, when the lines of people waiting at the communal neighborhood well stretched unbearably long, he carried buckets of water from the river to his home so that his family could cook and bathe. In the fall, when the autumn rain–filled river would flood the adjacent farm fields, sweeping pumpkins and other large vegetables downstream, Milan would pluck them out of the deluge and proudly take them home. In the winter, when the town lay buried under a mantle of snow and frost, he went to the shore to collect driftwood and drag it home to feed the fireplace that kept his family's cottage warm. The river always flowed on, whether swollen by floods, depleted by drought, or frozen by winter. Through the darkest times of his childhood, when Milan was faced with the miseries of a home run by a desperate, addicted, and outcast mother, he would contemplate the serene resolve of the river to move ever forward, and he found a similar resolution growing inside himself.

The river also taught him an important spiritual lesson. One year, the drought was particularly severe, and it devastated the community. The crops failed and the cattle starved. Faced with potential catastrophe, the town leaders united and rallied people of all the three major faiths (and some minor ones, too) to pray for rain to restore the waters. Milan watched as Orthodox, Catholics, Muslims, Jews, and others gathered on the withered banks of the depleted river. He heard the various forms of prayer—the different modes of entreaty and supplication—and watched as various religious leaders led their congregations in established worship rituals. Milan wondered whether anyone heard their pleas. Three days later, the rains returned, the river rose, and the people rejoiced. Someone had heard and answered the prayers. Milan did not know which of the groups, if any, had reached the Great Provider. But profoundly moved by the miracle, Milan cherished this memory for the rest of his life.

Church

Droning chants filled the sacred space, reverberating off the stone walls. Radiant icons looked on from behind the altar, inspiring the worshipers to express their reverence and devotion. Heady incense poured from a censer suspended on golden chains above the front of the nave, sanctifying both the space and its occupants.

Milan, dressed in the white-and-gold vestments of an acolyte, assisted the priest. He carried the candle to light the candlestick in front of the icon of Saint Sava and held up the prayer book from which the priest recited. Milan shifted from foot to foot under the heavy robes, still unused to this privileged position by the priest's side. Sweat trickled down his skin in the hot atmosphere. But despite his nervousness and discomfort, Milan faithfully remained at his post, holding up the heavy tome until his arms begin to cramp with fatigue. Milan knew that he was lucky to have been chosen by the priest and had resolved to do whatever it took to retain this prestigious position.

The time of sanctification arrived, and Milan brought the priest a portable censer that is swung toward the space, object, or person that is being sanctified. After sanctifying the congregation, the priest turned to face the sanctuary to sanctify the altar.

The solemn liturgy began, the congregation joined in to swell the prayer, and the priest swung the heavy censer. But one of the chains, worn down from years of use, broke at the peak of the swing. The censer fell, clattering loudly on the stone floor and spilling incense on the ground. Directly beside the priest, Milan heard him curse softly beneath his breath.

The words shocked the boy. Could it be true? Was the priest really cursing before the altar? Stunned, Milan looked up at him. The man appeared unchanged. His face still wore the pious, self-assured look of a spiritual leader. Milan's mind spun. He gripped the candle in his hands until they hurt. How could this be? How could a servant of God and a leader of His people curse so coarsely and casually? Milan glanced back at the congregation. They stood devoutly, having noticed or heard nothing, unaware that their worship leader had just uttered vile words in the presence of God.

Milan mechanically went through the remaining motions of the service. When it was finally over, he removed the vestments, folded them carefully, and put them away in the storage room. Then, without explanation, he told the priest that he was quitting his position and left the church without a backward glance, determined never to return to such hypocrisy.

* * * * *

This traumatic church experience was one of the most formative in Milan's childhood. After overcoming his mother's unbelief and his community's disapproval, he had dedicated himself at a young age to serve God. Though raised in ignorance of spiritual things, Milan felt a strong need to be of service and help in the church. This was a brave act for one so young, and he initially felt greatly rewarded when the priest made him an acolyte. For the first time, it seemed, Milan's life had meaning. By taking an active part in the church service, he was both helping his community and serving God.

All this came to an end when he overheard the priest's blasphemous curse. Milan could not reconcile that brazen act with the position of spiritual leadership and the carefully cultivated exterior of piousness. He knew that the community deeply respected the priest and his office. Milan knew what and whom the priest symbolized. The priest was a connection to the Divine, a representative of the Father. He was supposed to be an example to others, but instead, this priest was an unrepentant blasphemer, hiding under a facade of holiness. Such gross hypocrisy could not be borne.

After this experience, Milan turned his back on organized religion and the worldly forms of worship. He still hadn't figured it all out, but he knew that there was something inherently false in a religion where the leaders could and did curse with impunity in the house of God. This revelation would remain central to Milan for the rest of his life, and the disillusionment would eventually lead to a new understanding of what true, sincere religion is. But that would come much later. For the time being, Milan would seek God through the spirituality found in nature and in acts of kindness toward others. For now, organized religion held no worth to him.

CHAPTER TWO

WAR

Unless the L*ORD* *had given me help,*
I would soon have dwelt in the silence of death.
When I said, "My foot is slipping,"
your unfailing love, L*ORD*, *supported me.*
When anxiety was great within me,
your consolation brought me joy.

—Psalm 94:17–19

Threats

Milan raced up the street, his feet flying in fear over the cobblestones. He burst through the door of his home, startling his mother and sisters. They stared at him in wonder and apprehension.

"What is it now? Who is harassing you this time?" his mother asked. She was unusually sober and wore a clean dress. The house, too, was unusually tidy and clean. But Milan was too agitated to notice.

"It was Zeljko," he gasped as he tried to catch his breath.

His mother pulled out a chair from the dining table and motioned for him to sit. She handed him a glass of water.

"Here, take this and compose yourself," she said.

Milan nodded and obeyed. A few minutes later, after he had calmed down enough to gulp the water, he told his mother and sisters what had happened. His hands trembled.

"I was walking through the town square, just minding my business, when Zeljko came out of the tavern and grabbed me by the hair!"

His mother clutched her apron in horror.

"I didn't know what to do," continued Milan. "He was drunk, and I didn't want to aggravate him, so I stayed quiet. But this time was worse than before, much worse. He was boasting, talking about how the Nazis had captured the king's army and how those who sided with the Nazis would now be in charge. Then Zeljko started to talk about Jasenovac, the death camp where they are taking all the men. It doesn't matter whether they are from Orthodox, Muslim, Jewish, or Roma backgrounds. Zeljko said anyone who resists the Nazis will be taken. At this point, I tried to wriggle out of his grasp, but he just clamped down harder on my hair until I thought he would pull it out by the roots!"

The girls cried softly as they listened.

"I think he was expecting me to beg for mercy or something, because he got even madder when I said nothing in response to all his threats. He told me that he knew I had been spending the nights all month hiding in the forest and that I didn't need to worry because there was no need to send me to a death camp. He said he would take care of me himself and hang me from a lamppost by sundown."

Milan put his head in his hands and groaned softly. Though it was still early in the afternoon and the sun shone brightly through the windows, he felt as if his world were dark as midnight.

"So he thinks that now that the Nazis are here, he's a big shot, does he? Someone needs to straighten him out. I think it's time for a little talk with Zeljko."

Milan gaped at the tall, broad form that had materialized from the shadowed back room. It was Mato, his stepfather, unexpectedly back from his army service. Without a further word, Mato strode out of the house and headed straight for the center of town, clumping down the street in his heavy boots.

In the tavern, Mato immediately spotted Zeljko at a table full of rowdy, blustering village troublemakers. Mato dropped a heavy hand on Zeljko's shoulder.

"Come, brother, let us step out for a moment," he said quietly but firmly. "You look like you could use some fresh air to clear your head."

The sour look on Zeljko's face betrayed just how little he wanted to comply, but he had little choice in the matter. Mato was a powerful man who still wore the king's uniform even though the army had been disbanded. Together they left the noisy tavern.

Mato steered them to a back alley. Then he drew his pistol and pointed it straight at Zeljko's pale face.

"Listen very carefully," he said. "Leave my son alone. He is a good lad and does not deserve your abuse. If you bother him one more time, it will be you who will be hanging from a lamppost." With that, he left Zeljko in the alley, stunned and speechless.

When Mato returned home, the same hand that had dealt so harshly with Zeljko was gently laid on Milan's shoulder. "Don't worry, son. I have taken care of that troublemaker. He won't bother you anymore."

Overflowing with gratitude, Milan gave his stepfather a warm hug and buried his face in Mato's shoulder.

* * * * *

Milan's experience of Mato's unexpected intervention left him with two important life lessons. The first was never to generalize. Zeljko was from a Catholic background, and Milan was from an Orthodox one. The two sides had traditionally been enemies for centuries in Bosnia. This was, at least ostensibly, the reason why Zeljko had targeted Milan for abuse and even death. Milan could have let this traumatic experience prejudice him against Catholics. But how could he, when his stepfather and deliverer, Mato, was a Catholic himself? This was a particularly important lesson for a young Bosnian to learn while growing up in an environment marred by sectarian divisions and violence. In every major conflict, extremists would take advantage of the chaos to carry out massacres and ethnic cleansing. Many people fell for their lies and were drawn into the factional hatred. But early on, Milan learned that it was a person's heart and deeds, and not their ethnic group or religion, that defined and characterized them. Thus, he avoided the quagmire of prejudice that so many others sunk into.

The second lesson was that Providence would intervene in his life at the direst of times. Zeljko had been harassing Milan for weeks, but it was at the critical moment, when his life was in danger, that Mato providentially showed up to save him. This could not be ascribed to chance. After this experience, a profound conviction began to grow in Milan that God had spared him because He had a plan for Milan's life. This conviction would continue to grow and be strengthened by succeeding events that testified to God's care and His direct protection of Milan. And because he believed that God cared for and protected him, Milan would be led to conclude that it was his duty to gratefully serve and obey his divine Guardian. Thereby was the seed planted that would later sprout and flourish into a life devoted to mission.

Joining the Partisans

"Wake up, Milan; the soldiers are coming!"

Milan was shaken out of sleep. His mother bent over him and peered into his face to make sure that he was fully awake.

"What is it?" he asked thickly, his mind still sleepy.

"It's the soldiers. They are coming. Everyone is leaving town. Quick! We have to run!"

Instantly awake, Milan jumped to his feet and splashed his face with cold water out of the pail in the kitchen. He was used to this; they had needed to run away from town many times before. From beyond the cottage walls, the sounds of commotion could be clearly heard: people shouting, cattle bellowing, and wheels of wagons and carts clattering. His mother and sisters were busy securing their most precious belongings and what little food they could carry with them. Milan made himself helpful, collecting and tying up a bundle of split logs that he would carry to their hiding place in the mountains. It was midwinter, and keeping a fire going was vital for survival.

"Which army is it this time?" he asked sullenly. "Is it the Ustashe or the Chetniks, those bloodthirsty local murderers who come to take our men to the death camps? Or is it the Nazis or the Fascists, those foreign invaders who work us to death building roads for their artillery?"

"I have no idea," his mother said distractedly, rushing about to make sure she hadn't forgotten anything important. "What does it matter, anyhow? One side is as bad as the other."

Having finished their packing, the family moved toward the door to leave. But then Vida noticed the sounds outside had ceased. An eerie silence had fallen on the town.

"Why are you waiting?" Milan asked. "We must go. There is no time to lose."

"Shh," his mother said, placing a finger over her lips.

The girls moved softly to the window to see what was going on. Milan protectively pulled them away but then could not resist the urge himself and crouched below the window, peering out from beneath the curtain's fringe. The street was deathly still. No one could be seen where a few moments before all was astir. Only the traces in the snow attested to the recent commotion.

They waited there for some time, moments that felt like centuries, until finally, the spell was broken by the tramp of feet marching down the street. But something was wrong. Unlike the disciplined, measured tread of the various armies that had previously occupied their town, this march was broken and irregular. It sounded like no army they had heard before. Then the soldiers came into view. They looked different from other soldiers Milan had seen. They were wearing either civilian clothing or the uniforms of the other armies with their badges torn off. Half of them didn't have weapons, and more than half didn't have boots. In their ranks, Milan spotted familiar faces: the Orthodox banker who used to work in the town square, a priest from the Catholic church, a Muslim plumber from a nearby neighborhood, and many others. Joining in the march at the rear of the column were civilians who had lost their fear and were following the procession to the center of town.

Vida opened the door, and they followed the throng to the town square. There, the captain of the army spoke from a wooden platform.

He spoke of freedom from oppression, of repelling the invaders and subduing the local oppressors alike. He talked about the common people, their oppression under the aristocrats, and their worth to society. The captain was dressed in civilian clothes, but he had a brand-new Nazi rifle slung over his back and wore a cap with a red star. He was the leader of this band of Partisans.

At the end of the speech, the captain told the listening townspeople that they were safe now that the guerilla fighters held the roads around Derventa and would ambush any approaching force, whether of Ustashe or Chetniks, Nazis or Fascists. The people cheered with joy and cried with relief. Then the captain invited all the remaining able-bodied men to join the guerillas in their quest to liberate Bosnia. Milan watched as many of the men of Derventa moved through the crowd to the front. Beside him, his childhood friend Marko moved forward as well.

"Where are you going?" Milan asked in surprise. "We are too young to fight."

"No," Marko replied, his jaw set determinedly. "I am too old to hide anymore."

Milan looked at his mother with a clear question in his eyes. She nodded, hugged him fiercely, and then pushed him forward.

"Go," she whispered. "Join the freedom fighters and liberate our homeland from our enemies."

* * * * *

Like so many other key decisions in his life, joining the Partisans was a choice that Milan later would believe was guided by God. At the time, his future was very uncertain. He was a sixteen-year-old boy lost in a brutal world of upheaval and war. The army he joined was similarly lost, a ragtag group fighting against several armies of professional, well-trained, and fully equipped butchers. But both Milan and the Partisans would prevail against seemingly impossible odds. He would come to the logical conclusion that God had meant for him to join the side that would win the conflict in their local theater of the Second World War.

From an ethical perspective, the choice of joining the Partisans was the best. The Ustashe and the Chetniks were fundamentally selfish, nationalistic groups whose myopic aims were to wipe each other out and cleanse the land of their closest kin—each other. The Nazis and Fascists were totalitarian invaders seeking to establish great empires and subdue other peoples. But the Partisans, at least at the start, were motivated by a desire to empower the common people and bring peace to the land. Eventually, they would become a key part, though somewhat overlooked, of the Allied host that defeated the Axis powers in Europe. Milan faced a critical question: Which side would he join? In the future, he would always believe that God had led him to join the least objectionable and bloodthirsty of the armies. But soon, he would learn that even this right choice came at a terrible cost.

A river crossing

The night was pitch black under heavy clouds. A small band of Partisans hurried through the forest on their way to meet with other units for a coordinated attack on a Nazi convoy. But that was not the only reason for their haste. According to the scouts, behind them was a small group of Chetnik snipers, too small to openly attack but not too small to pick off stragglers at the end of the line.

Milan was close to the rear. Whenever a break in the clouds permitted the moon to shine through, he heard the soft whiz of bullets and the thuds of dead men falling to the ground. When the gloom returned, some of the bolder Chetniks tackled stragglers and finished them off with knives. But the Partisan band hurried on to its destination, never stopping to engage their attackers. Above all else, the mission must succeed. Milan sensed the danger of his position at the rear and took advantage of his youth to increase his speed. He jumped over fallen branches and took shortcuts over higher ground. When he was about halfway up the line of marching men, Milan fell back into the ranks.

There he felt slightly safer, though danger still lurked behind.

They approached a river. Like most rivers in Bosnia, this one was fed by hill streams and was swift and perilous. The enemy held all the bridges in this area, so the Partisans were forced to ford the river in a remote and dangerous place. There were rapids immediately downstream from where they planned to cross, so if anyone lost their footing and fell, they would be swept away instantly.

Many of the men could not swim. A couple of them proposed holding hands, but the commander instantly shut down this idea.

"What do you think this is, a nursery?" he snapped gruffly. "What needs to be in your hands is your rifle, not a weakling's hand. Hold your weapons high above the waters. The success of our mission and our survival depends on our guns."

They waded into the chilly, surging water. Milan had no trouble. Having spent so many childhood days in the Ukrina River, he knew how to make his way sure-footedly across the unknown riverbed. Furthermore, Milan was free from the paralyzing fear that grips those who cannot swim. If he fell, Milan knew that he could rely on his excellent swimming skills to survive.

Halfway across the dark river, the comrade behind him slipped and fell with a fearful cry. Instinctively, Milan turned to help. He was about to cast away his rifle and dive after the man when he felt a hard hand seize him by the arm.

"Don't even think of it," said an even harder voice. It was the sergeant. "You heard the commander. We go forward and keep our guns dry, no matter the cost."

With a chill in his heart to match the chill of the river water, Milan forded the rest of the river and climbed the far bank to safety. His gun was dry, and so were his arms that he held far up above the water. But the rest of him was soaked to the bone. Putting his gun aside, Milan hugged himself and started to rock back and forth on the ground as chills seized him. Some of the men muttered about starting a fire to warm up and dry their clothes.

"Absolutely not!" the commander raged. "Have you fools forgotten the Chetnik snipers behind us? What do you think they will do when they see us lounging in plain view by the fire? Join us for dinner? We'll be shot on the spot. Now get going. We will march ourselves dry."

On through the gloom Milan marched, the wet clothes clinging to his shivering body. He kept thinking about the man who had been behind him, swept away by the waters into the merciless rapids. Milan knew he could have pulled him from his death and saved him. In Milan's mind, the last, desperate cry of the man kept ringing. The darkness of the night was great, but the darkness in his soul was greater still.

* * * * *

At the time, Milan could see little more than the darkness in this tragic river crossing. All he could think about was the brutal, heartless way in which a man's life was sacrificed so that a war strategy could be carried out successfully.

However, over time, Milan came to reflect on his own deliverance. He could have easily ended up like that man. If Milan had not spent all that time at the Ukrina River, unwittingly training for the future, he never would have become so skilled at being in the water and quite likely would have drowned. To be sure, Milan was forever sorrowful about the fate of his abandoned comrade. But he also learned to thank God for preparing him for that dark hour through innocent childhood games. Once again, the almighty hand of Providence had directed Milan on a path that kept him safe and ensured his survival.

Eventually, this and other events that displayed the protecting role of God in his life would lead Milan to a profound understanding that he had been spared for a reason. He was being trained by life struggles for a higher calling. God had a plan for him, and He was ensuring that His servant would live through deadly perils to fulfill a divine purpose. Soon, the day would arrive when Milan would discover this great purpose. Then all the past events would be made clear, and all the terrible tragedies surrounding him would make sense in light of God's grand plan for his life.

Trapped

The little band of Partisans camped in an open field by a brook that chattered noisily through reeds and stones. The guerillas were worn out from long marches and desperate fighting. Most of them were stretched out on their backs, instantly asleep upon hitting the ground. A single sentry was stationed in the direction of the dense forest that curved around the field and crossed the brook both up and downstream. By the fire, Milan and Marko, the youngest Partisans, were cooking a stew whose ingredients were donated by villagers along their march. The youths were tired; Milan kept dropping the ladle into the stew, and Marko had to slap himself to stay awake.

They were both brought wide awake by a low birdcall from the sentry. He motioned to them to keep quiet and then pointed in the direction where the forest crossed the brook upstream.

"Look," the sentry said softly, after crawling over to them. "Can you see them? There are a couple of Nazi soldiers by the brook."

Sure enough, Milan and Marko could see the soldiers. They seemed to be intently observing the Partisan band.

"What should we do?" Marko whispered. "Wake up the rest and capture the enemy?"

"Look," Milan said, pointing in the opposite direction downstream. "There are more of them."

Sure enough, another pair of Nazis were stationed at the other side of the field. They were also staring intently at the band.

"We need to move quickly," Marko said, "if we want to capture both groups before they alert their division and bring them all down on our heads."

"Oh no," groaned the sentry. "Look over at the far side of the field."

Milan and Marko followed his pointing hand that shook with fear. The forest was full of Nazis! There were at least a hundred of them, hiding behind bushes and trees, their rifles aimed right at the unsuspecting band. They easily outnumbered the Partisans two to one.

Without a further word, Milan moved swiftly to the sole foxhole that had been dug in the soft soil by the brook. In it slept the radio operator with his transistor. Milan shook him awake and quickly informed him of the situation. The man's face paled, and his hands shook like the sentry's, but he immediately placed a call to the nearest Partisan band. There was no response. He kept trying, but no voice of assurance responded to let them know help was on the way.

"Is that it?" Milan asked. "Are we lost?"

The operator shrugged. "Maybe," he said. "All the transistors we have were taken from the enemy in battle, so sometimes the radio is broken so that they can only receive but not return messages. And sometimes it is completely broken. We will soon find out."

Milan scrambled out of the foxhole to alert the others but found his work already done. Marko and the sentry had awakened everyone. The Partisans still lay on the ground, but now they were on their bellies, wide awake and facing an encircling enemy. Milan dropped to the ground and crawled over to Marko.

"Why don't we try to cross the brook?" he suggested. "That way, we put the water between the enemy and us as we retreat."

"There are Nazis on the other side as well. We are completely surrounded."

Whispers began to circulate among the men. They contained the commander's orders:

"We have radioed for help. There is no response. Whether we receive aid or not, this is where we make our stand. There will be no retreat. We will fight until the end."

Bullets began whistling overhead. The Nazis were closing in. The Partisans held their fire, saving their last few bullets for the final enemy charge. As Milan held his rifle close, he could feel his heart beating like a drum. Sweat poured from his palms and face. The world somehow became both vivid and remote at the same time as he went into prebattle shock.

Suddenly, a strange calm swept over him. His heart quieted, and the sweat cooled on his skin. Before he knew what he was doing, he had dropped his rifle and was kneeling in the field.

"Milan, get down!" hissed Marko. "Have you lost your mind? You are an obvious target."

Oblivious to everything around him, Milan prayed.

"Dear God," he said. "I don't know what Your plan is. But if it is Your will, please deliver us from our enemies."

Then he was slammed to the ground by Marko. Bullets and shells shrieked overhead. The shouts of advancing Nazi officers could be heard, urging their men forward. Then, the enemy suddenly fell silent. The bullets stopped hailing around them. Instead, Milan heard the Partisans cheering.

Raising his head, he was greeted with an incredible sight: from behind the Nazi ranks, a much larger host was attacking. It was another band of Partisans, who had encircled the first circle of Nazis. By seeking to set a trap, their enemies had fallen into one themselves. Now the Nazis had to fight Partisans on both sides. Their ranks were spread so thin that the fight was over in mere minutes. Milan and Marko staggered up in disbelief, barely able to accept their deliverance.

"What are you two doing?" snapped the sergeant. "Get back to the cooking pot! If I find that you let the stew burn, you'll both be eating grass for dinner."

* * * * *

This deliverance experience built on the previous one by the Ukrina River, when Milan had witnessed the townspeople of various faiths praying for a miracle to end the drought. Both times God answered the prayers. He delivered the town from drought with rainfall, and He delivered the trapped band by sending another larger force of Partisans. The difference was that the first time, Milan witnessed others praying, while the second time, he had prayed. Milan had moved from observing to initiating.

No longer was God someone who was sought by others. Now Milan had a direct connection to the great Deliverer. Now he knew that God listened to his prayers as well. This was a lesson that Milan would take with him on his journey through life. As he was faced with numerous other trials, Milan would find himself, time and again, praying for deliverance to the God who had entrapped the entrappers. God had delivered Milan before, and He would deliver Milan again.

The suicide mission

As the war neared its end, the Nazis retreated as the Partisans slowly pushed them out of northern Bosnia, bitterly contesting every inch. At the strategically positioned town of Nova Topola, the northern gateway from Croatia into Bosnia, Milan's band waged a desperate battle to dislodge the entrenched enemy. Most of the town was retaken after a series of bitter, grueling fights in the ruined buildings of the devastated town. But the key position was still held by the Nazis. Right at the heart of town, where the main road ran by the square, the enemies had fortified a solidly built church. The Partisans attacked with their full force until the enemies were pushed back and holed up in the sanctuary. At the top of the bell tower, the Nazis placed a veteran machine gunner with a seemingly inexhaustible supply of ammunition. From his position, he commanded a 360-degree sweep of the surrounding courtyard. No one could approach without being mowed down. And thanks to the terrible toll in lives that the urban warfare took on the Partisans, they lacked the numbers to attack from multiple angles. The commander decided to try a desperate tactic.

Calling the two youngest Partisans, who also happen to be the fastest and smallest, the commander gave them their orders. The first would run at the church from the back, while the other attacked from the front. They were each given a rifle and grenade. Whoever survived the dash was to take out the holed-up Nazis and the machine gunner. The two young Partisans were Marko and Milan.

There was no time to say goodbye. Marko went to his position at the back of the church. He charged first. The machine gunner swung around and cut him down halfway across the courtyard. Milan, running for his life, made it to the church. He was beneath the bell tower, too low for the machine gunner's deadly reach. Milan burst into the church and hurled his grenade. Something stung his left leg in the calf muscle, but Milan was too hyped on adrenaline and fear to notice. As the smoke cleared from the broken pews, he could see that all the Nazis were dead. Milan moved to the base of the bell tower and finished off the machine gunner with a single rifle shot. Outside he heard his comrades cheering, but inside, all Milan felt was a terrible, hollow sadness—for the dead young men, Partisans and Nazis alike, caught up in a conflict that wrested them from their homes and destroyed their lives in their prime; for the dead civilians, casualties of a struggle for power and possession; and for Marko, sacrificed so that Milan could live and kill.

And then he felt something else. As the adrenaline and fear subsided, a growing pain began to spread upward. Milan looked down. His left pant leg was soaked crimson. His boot sloshed with blood at every step. The pain overpowered him like a black tide, and Milan fell—out of the nightmare of war and into the blessed oblivion of unconsciousness.

* * * * *

The battle of Topola was the last one that Milan fought. His wound was not particularly severe, but the lack of proper medical services in the war-torn region meant subpar treatment. His leg took a long time to heal, and he returned home to Derventa to convalesce.

There, he was treated as a hero. The Partisans had won the struggle between the various factions that had battled to expel the foreign invaders and gain control of Bosnia and the surrounding south Slav regions. They were poised to take and hold power. And the battle of Nova Topola further solidified the Partisans' position at the top. So Milan belonged to the winning side and was viewed as someone who had helped liberate the people from foreign invaders and local oppressors.

But he did not feel like a hero. All he had done was what he had to do to survive. For that, he was thankful to God and not to his own bravery or strength. And that was not all. His survival meant that he had watched others die. Not only that, but he had also killed many men. As he lay in his bed, racked by pain and guilt, the countless deaths he had witnessed came back to his mind. Instead of basking in the glow of victory and societal esteem, Milan was tortured by the past. He knew that his survival had been contingent on the deaths of others. Gradually, he began to lose sight of God's protecting hand and could only focus on the dark hand of death that had taken so many lives.

And finally, his disordered mind began to brood on his own role, and he saw himself now as an agent of destruction and chaos. It did not matter whose side he was on. All that mattered was that he had destroyed and killed. Amid this inner turmoil and personal darkness, he forgot how Providence had intervened on his behalf, how his life had been spared for a greater purpose, and how he had no choice but to fight to stay alive. Despair consumed him, and he turned to the vices that had plagued his mother. He began to smoke cigarettes and neglected his budding relationship with God. Just as he was starting to find his true path to the Father, Milan strayed and became lost. It was only after the horrors of the war had ended that the darkest chapter in his life took place. He had survived the war in the physical sense, but in the spiritual sense, he had died. It would take a rebirth, a resurrection of the spirit, to restore him to the care and guidance of God.

CHAPTER THREE

DARKNESS

The Lord makes firm the steps
of the one who delights in him;
though he may stumble, he will not fall,
for the Lord upholds him with his hand.

I was young and now I am old,
yet I have never seen the righteous forsaken
or their children begging bread.
They are always generous and lend freely;
their children will be a blessing.

—Psalm 37:23–26

A refusal

It was springtime, and the whole town was rejoicing. In all the main streets and especially in the square, the townspeople celebrated the end of the war and the Partisan victory. They danced the *kolo*, a fast-paced, traditional south Slav dance in which the dancers link in a circle with their arms draped around one another's waists. Songs about the Partisans' glorious victories echoed in the streets and floated down from open windows. Slogans were chanted, many of which contained the words written on red banners hung all over town: Brotherhood and Unity! Tables had been set out and piled high with food and drink. Delicious smells mingled with the sound of merriment as the revelers feasted and regaled one another with tales of the Partisans' bravery and accomplishments.

As Milan made his way through the festive throngs, many hailed him. They called him a hero and saluted him. His progress was slow, not only because of his limp but also because people constantly stopped him, wanting to shake his hand, thump him on the back, or embrace him. He was invited to eat at every table he passed. However, he politely declined even though his heart was full of happiness. The dark thoughts that assailed him during his convalescence seemed to have been banished in the light of day and the celebration of the grateful townspeople. Derventa was free and at peace again, and it was thanks to Milan's and his comrades' efforts.

In the grand, gray building that housed the mayor's office, Milan walked up a broad staircase, dragging his healed but atrophied leg up one step at a time. On the third floor, he was greeted by a peasant woman dressed in blue, the color of the working class of the newly established Socialist Federal Republic of Yugoslavia. Limping, he followed her down a spacious hallway to great oaken doors that opened into the mayor's office. The office was lavishly furnished: an ornate chandelier hung from the ceiling, a huge desk commanded leather chairs, and the walls proudly displayed the tricolor Yugoslav flag with a superimposed red star, flanked by portraits of prominent revolutionary ideologists.

"Welcome, comrade!" the mayor boomed, rising from behind his desk. He gestured with an open palm. "Please, take a seat."

Milan blinked in surprise. The last time he had seen this man, they were both in a ditch, starving and freezing, covered in dirt and blood, pulling their helmets low as an artillery barrage thundered around them. Now he was round and aglow with good living, wearing an expensive suit with a red star pinned to his lapel.

The mayor offered Milan a cigarette, and they both smoked, a habit they had picked up during the harrowing days of the war and that they had retained, though the danger had passed. They made small talk while the worker in blue prepared coffee and brought it to them. Then the mayor dismissed her and told her to close the door.

"I have called you up here, Milan," he began, lighting another cigarette, "because you are needed. As you know, many of our men were lost during the war, and there are only a few who have proven themselves to be true revolutionaries. You are one of these. You fought bravely through the war up until you played a key role in the liberation of Nova Topola. The Party remembers and appreciates your service. And now the time for your reward has come."

"Thank you," answered Milan, staring down at the floor. He didn't know what to say. He didn't feel like a hero or like he had earned anything. He had just done what he needed to do to survive.

"Our town is being rebuilt," the mayor carried on through a cloud of tobacco smoke. "There will be new industries, owned by the people and run by proven revolutionaries who are faithful to our cause. We need men we can trust. Men like you."

"Thank you," Milan repeated, "but I am afraid that I am not qualified for a leadership position. I have very little formal education. In fact, I only went to primary school for a few years."

The mayor laughed loud and long until the laugh ended in a hacking cough. He put out his cigarette in an overflowing ashtray and leaned forward over the desk, staring intently at Milan.

"Don't concern yourself with such trifles. We made Darko head of the bank only last week, and he was a cow herder before the war. What counts is loyalty to the cause. All you need to do is join the Party, and everything will be taken care of. Everyone knows what a great hero you are. They are just waiting for you to openly declare your allegiance to the revolution and take a position of power. What do you say?"

Milan bit his lip and said nothing. He felt a little sick, and not just from all the cigarette smoke in the room.

"Think about it," said the mayor, leaning back in his opulent leather chair. "A big house and a bigger salary. An office like mine. A life of privilege and wealth. And all for a good cause: Brotherhood and Unity!"

Milan rubbed his chin thoughtfully and said, "Thank you again for your generous offer. It is really kind of you to remember me. But I must refuse. When I joined the Partisans, I did so to liberate our people, not to gain a position for which I am not qualified. You have mentioned Darko, and I have heard of many others like him. They are war heroes, of that there can be no doubt. But they are not administrators and leaders. They are simply men who were lucky enough to survive the horrors of war. And I am the same. I will find some humble work that befits my capabilities. Good day to you, comrade."

And with that, Milan rose and limped out of the office, leaving in his wake a shocked mayor.

* * * * *

There were two main reasons for Milan's refusal. The first was that he was deeply suspicious of positions of power, especially those held by people who were not qualified to hold them. His integrity was a virtue that he deeply valued, and he feared it would be compromised if he took a post solely because he had fought on the winning side in the war. He had watched other people ascend to positions they had no business holding. And he had seen how power corrupted them and turned them into less than what they were before. He resolved to resist temptation and to remain at his appropriate level.

The second reason was the ruling Party's hostility toward God. At this point in his life, Milan had degenerated into agnosticism. He questioned the existence of a God in the face of so many horrible war atrocities. But he could not support the strident antagonism of the new regime toward religion. Milan knew how corrupt the churches could be. After all, he had witnessed at an early age the hypocrisy of the priest who had cursed in the middle of a church service. This made him very pessimistic about organized religion.

But he never hated God, nor did he think that all religion should be abolished and that religious people should be persecuted. This was something he could not be a part of as a member of the unequivocally atheistic Party. So he turned down a life of ease and privilege for a life of hardship and disadvantage. But his mind was at peace, knowing that he had done the right thing.

A traumatic flashback

The atmosphere was oppressive and noisome, full of heat and the stench of melted metal. A cacophony of shrieks, groans, and grumbles of machinery filled the factory with a ceaseless din. Amid a profusion of workers toiling away in this industrial setting, Milan stood at his workstation, bent over a machine to bore and grind metal cylinders into rifle barrels. He was drenched in sweat and grimed with the fumes and soot of the factory, but he didn't mind. The hard work took his mind off other, far more unpleasant things. In fact, ever since he had started this factory job, he had been able to sleep deeply, exhausted by the work. He was satisfied—this was honest work that he felt qualified for. It was infinitely more suited to him than sitting in an office and ordering others around. And the mental focus it required kept his war memories repressed and out of the way.

A pealing bell signaled break time. Milan had started to make his way to the rest station with the others when he was waylaid by a supervisor.

"Come with me," the supervisor said. "The bosses are impressed with your work. They want to show you something."

Milan followed the supervisor through a labyrinth of machines and parts. They climbed several flights of metal stairs to the factory's offices. There, after wiping his greasy, calloused hands on a rag, Milan was greeted by a couple of large men in suits. They were beaming at him.

"Ah, here is our war hero! Welcome, Milan," they said, gripping him by the hand. "We have heard of your wartime exploits and of your humbleness in taking this post. You are a true model of a soldier and worker of the revolution!"

Milan bowed his head in humility.

"I have received reports of your excellent skill as a machinist," one of the men rumbled. "It seems that you are as skilled with machines as you are with weapons."

The others voiced their assent and continued to beam at Milan.

"We want to show you the finished result of your work. Here, take a look at this. This is the finished product."

From a rack on a sidewall, one of the men took down a rifle. It was finely crafted and gleamed with newness. It was placed in Milan's hands.

Instantly, the gun morphed in his mind. The bright, clean metal appeared dull and stained. Then the rest of the world followed suit. The factory was gone. Milan stood in a barren field full of wounded and dying men. Some of them were his friends, men he had been defending and trying to save. Others were his enemies, men he had been attacking and trying to kill. All were broken now, some irreparably so. Loathing and nausea welled up in him as the stench of death assailed his nostrils. Blood pounded in his temples. He gasped for breath, unable to fill his lungs with oxygen. Shaking with terror, he dropped the old, battered rifle. It clattered on the office floor, restored to the pristine, prized rifle of the factory.

Faces crowded around Milan to ask what the problem was and to splash his face with water. Eventually, the panic subsided, and he was able to breathe again. When he recovered enough to talk, he made an excuse about overworking and deflected their more penetrating questions. The bosses gave him the day off and told him to get some rest. Shaken by the traumatic flashback, Milan headed home. It seemed that the past wouldn't be buried that easily.

* * * * *

This experience was the first of many like it. Flashback followed flashback until Milan found that he was unable to work in the arms factory. Surrounded by parts of weapons and taking an active role in manufacturing them, he was engulfed by memories of the atrocities of war. Things got so bad that he had to quit and look for another job. But this meant that the exhaustion and focus of the work were gone. Now, the memories had free rein to return to torment him—and they did. He began to suffer continuously. During the day and the night, whether he opened his eyes or closed them, he saw the faces of the stricken or deceased. The horrors of the war returned to him with even greater force than their initial impression. Having no other solace, he began to smoke heavily and brood in solitude. This affected his ability to find a new job, and soon he spent most of his time alone at home, reflecting on the countless atrocities he had witnessed and wallowing in the insubstantial and fleeting shelter of substance abuse. And he had almost completely forgotten the God who had saved him so many times before. What was to become of him, a young man of about twenty who had survived a brutal war but could not escape the mental agonies of the past?

At the bottom

One day, Milan sat alone in a darkened room, smoking and brooding. The frown graven into his face showed that his heart was weighed down by dark thoughts. His fingers were stained yellow, and his breath reeked from the ceaseless tobacco smoking. From time to time, he gritted his teeth at the rooster crowing in the yard outside. Why wouldn't that dumb bird be quiet?

After leaving his machinist job at the weapons factory, Milan had withdrawn to his childhood home. His depression, already severe thanks to the traumatic recollections of the atrocities of the war, had deepened with what he witnessed of the postwar era. He used to have lofty ideals—grand plans and hopes for the revolutionary society the Partisans had fought to establish. It was to be founded on brotherhood and unity, justice and trust. The rooster crowed again, and the sound pierced Milan's already aching head. Cursing, he flung the ashtray at the back door, spilling its contents all over the floor. But this only added chicken squawks to the din. Milan clutched his head and lit yet another cigarette.

The dark thoughts continued. Instead of the ideals he had fought for, Milan now saw all sorts of new atrocities and injustices happening within their new society. A former commander of an Ustashe unit, a brutal man who had filled several mass graves with women, children, and the elderly, was caught by the people, tied upside down to a pole, and planted with his head in an anthill. At the same time, other war criminals who had committed crimes of the same magnitude had escaped punishment and walked freely in broad daylight simply because they had connections to the ruling party. Was this the justice Milan had fought for? Was this the new society his comrades had died for?

The rooster crowed again and flapped his wings right outside the window. Milan smashed a chair against the wall, thinking, *That should shut the dumb bird up.*

He returned to his dark thoughts. People were disappearing. The first to disappear were those who had not joined the Party and who did not have a record of service during the war to redeem them as Milan did. One evening they would be with their families as usual, and the next morning they would be gone forever, whisked away in the night by the secret police. Then it got worse. Anyone who had enemies in power was at risk. Milan knew several of his neighbors had disappeared. All of them had issues with those in power, whether based on jealousy, long-held grudges, or merely sadistic whims. How could this be the glorious new community for which the freedom fighters had sacrificed their health and lives?

The rooster crowed directly in front of the door, as if in a brazen affront to Milan's headache and depression. Something in him snapped. He jumped to his feet and stomped out of the house. A few minutes later, he returned and resumed his seat. He sat there for a while, staring at nothing, his mind as empty as his hopes. Then he wiped his hand on his pants to clean it of the blood and feathers and lit a cigarette. Outside, there was no sound from the rooster.

* * * * *

This period of depression—the lowest point in Milan's life—was symptomatic of a deeper cause than the wartime and postwar atrocities he had witnessed. In his heart of hearts, Milan longed to know God, the true judge and founder of an ideal society. As a boy, Milan had encountered God's blessings and protection, but during and after the war, he lost his way and forgot that his life was part of the divine plan. So, his life fell apart: his smoking turned into a vile yet indispensable crutch, his temper flared at the slightest provocation, and he lost the ability to relate to and tolerate others, which forced him into self-imposed isolation. And he brooded endlessly on the horrors of the war and the horrors of the dystopia he had helped create, without the merciful intervention of a heavenly hope. Down at the bottom of this pit of despair, Milan could see no light to show him a way out. All seemed hopeless and lost.

But God was not done with him. There was still hope for Milan, and soon this lost lamb would be found by the great Shepherd and restored to the path that leads ever upward.

CHAPTER FOUR

INTO THE LIGHT

I love the LORD, *for he heard my voice;*
he heard my cry for mercy.
Because he turned his ear to me,
I will call on him as long as I live.

The cords of death entangled me,
the anguish of the grave came over me;
I was overcome by distress and sorrow.
Then I called on the name of the LORD:
*"*LORD, *save me!"*

The LORD *is gracious and righteous;*
our God is full of compassion.
The LORD *protects the unwary;*
when I was brought low, he saved me.

Return to your rest, my soul,
for the LORD *has been good to you.*

For you, LORD, *have delivered me from death,*
my eyes from tears,
my feet from stumbling,
that I may walk before the LORD
in the land of the living.

—Psalm 116:1–9

A meeting

Milan walked through the streets of the town in the twilight. He was tired from hours and hours of walking aimlessly. He hadn't found work yet, and his restlessness drove him out of the house in search of something unknown. Milan's leg began to ache. The war wound was acting up again, as it usually did after one of these long treks. He decided to stop by the pharmacy on his way home to get some medicine.

The pharmacy was in an old building, but the interior had been carefully maintained. Everything was clean and orderly: there wasn't a speck of dust on the counter, and the few medicine bottles on the shelves were carefully arranged and labeled. Behind the counter stood a young woman. She was neatly dressed and wore a prominent crucifix. She smiled kindly at Milan when he entered, but he was immediately struck by her gravity and composure.

"Good evening," she said. "How can I help you?"

"It's my leg," he told her. "It's been bothering me more than usual lately."

He rolled up his pant leg to show her the wound. It had been leaking again and was inflamed. She came around the counter for a closer look. Composed and calm, she inspected the wound.

"I was hoping I could get some ointment," Milan said, "to help it heal and keep the swelling down."

"Yes," she agreed. "That is what you need. But, unfortunately, we are out of ointment right now. However, I can make some using natural ingredients, if you don't mind waiting for a little bit."

While the young woman put together a home remedy for his wound, Milan took a seat and helped himself to some tea that had been set out for customers. She was clearly competent—selecting the various herbs and substances with assurance and mashing them together with a mortar and pestle. As she worked, she asked Milan about the wound and how he got it. But he was hesitant to speak of the past.

"It was a bad time," he said. "I saw many terrible things done and did some terrible things too. I would rather not talk about them."

"I understand," she replied. "Though I didn't take part in any of the fighting, I still saw some of the horrors of the war and had to deal with everyday hardships."

To take Milan's mind off the wound and his bad memories, the young woman shared her stories. She told him of the struggles to provide proper treatment and medicines during the many blockades and sieges of the town. She spoke of the senior pharmacists (at that time, she was just an apprentice) vanishing one by one, some taken by force to treat various war bands, some lost in despair to alcohol. Eventually, she was left all alone to tend to the needs of the whole town.

"It was a hard time," she said as she wrapped up his treated wound with expert hands. "But my faith in God saw me through it all."

She reverently touched her crucifix. Milan nodded and said nothing. His faith was gone, but he didn't want to say anything to insult this kind, capable person. As he left, he suddenly remembered something.

"I'm sorry," he said, back at the counter. "But I have been terribly rude. You have helped me and shared your experiences with me, and I never bothered to introduce myself. My name is Milan."

"Nice to meet you, Milan," she said while smiling and shaking his hand. "My name is Anka. Whenever you need help with the wound, don't hesitate to stop by."

* * * * *

Meeting Anka was an extremely important development in Milan's life. At the time, because of his psychological problems dealing with the aftermath of the war, he had become almost completely isolated and withdrawn. Making a friend was the first step toward his eventual recovery. In the succeeding weeks, Milan returned to the pharmacy for more medicine and to have his wound dressed.

They grew closer with each visit, and Milan began to realize how pleasant it was to be around another person. And Anka was a positive influence on him. She did not smoke, and he felt ashamed of his own habit when he was in her presence. She was faithful, and as a result of her Christian beliefs, she was charitable to those in need, those like Milan. This made a deep impression on him. He had encountered so many godless and selfish people during and after the war that he had almost forgotten that some lived to serve others. Anka was one of them. Through her friendship and care, Milan began to feel the influence of God in his life once again. Thus, they began a journey together that would continue through the years.

On the promenade

It was twilight, and Milan was out walking again, but this time it wasn't through empty streets but on the promenade in the center of town, among the well-dressed socialites and near the many aromatic eateries and snug cafés. And this time, he wasn't alone. Beside him walked Anka, and behind them were two of her older sisters, acting as chaperones.

Milan and Anka made small talk, admiring the yellow, orange, and red hues of the autumn leaves and basking in the mild weather. Then Anka steered their conversation to more serious matters.

"Tell me," she said, "about your work. What do you do these days?"

Milan frowned. "When the war was over and I returned to Derventa, I was offered a high position by the mayor, a former comrade of mine. But I turned it down because I felt that I was not qualified for the job."

Anka nodded. "The town is full of people holding offices they never earned. This causes many problems. You did the right thing."

"Thank you," Milan said gratefully. "After that," he continued, "I went to Sarajevo to work as a machinist at a weapons factory. The work was hard, but I enjoyed it and, if I may say so, did pretty well. But being surrounded by all those weapons brought back many terrible memories from the war. All the past horrors came flooding back, sometimes in uncontrollable and overwhelming flashbacks. I couldn't handle it, so I quit."

He hung his head in shame. Anka patted him on the shoulder and said nothing, knowing that sometimes the best reassurance is expressed in silence.

After a pause, Milan concluded, "Now I am looking for work. It isn't easy, because all the bosses know how I turned down the leadership position, and many of them consider me an ungrateful fool. Plus, word has spread about my problems in Sarajevo. Who wants to hire a worker whose nightmares can be triggered by a piece of metal?"

Having reached the end of the promenade, the two of them turned around to retrace their steps. They passed by Anka's sisters, who smiled cordially at Milan but appraised him with a critical eye. They had heard conflicting stories about him, as had Anka. Some of the stories were about his bravery and fighting prowess during the war. Others were about his social isolation and work problems.

"But even though I have no work," said Milan, "I still stay busy. My mother works very hard all day, and when she returns home, she is usually too tired to cook or clean. So, I do all the household chores and care for my two younger sisters."

Anka smiled sadly. "I can relate," she said. "My mother died not long after giving birth to my youngest sibling, and my father, a mason, comes home almost too exhausted to speak, much like your mother. There are ten of us, nine sisters and one brother. As one of the oldest, I have my hands full taking care of the little ones." She laughed. "You should see what it's like on Sunday morning when I have to bathe and dress the whole troop for church. Working at the pharmacy is a breeze compared to that!"

Milan suddenly stiffened. A tension, which had been repressed so far in their relationship, resurfaced slightly. "I'm afraid I don't know much about preparing for church, or going to it, for that matter. It has been a long time since I set foot in the house of God, and I don't plan on doing so anytime soon."

Anka's face was expressionless, but beneath, doubt and worry seethed.

Milan sensed he had not chosen his words well. "I am sorry," he said. "I meant no offense. When I was young, I had a bad experience with a priest who cursed during a church service. Since then, I have not been to church."

"That's OK," Anka reassured him. "Whether you go to church or not, you can still love God and pray to Him. As you know, my family is Polish, and we don't exactly fit into the congregation or always get along with our fellow believers. But I still trust in God and pray to Christ. It is a great comfort to know that there is Someone who cares about and comforts me."

Milan nodded politely but did not reply. His heart was in turmoil as he pondered Anka's words. Despite his own doubt, he could not help but admire her faith. Her words awakened something in his heart that had lain dormant for a long time. Feelings that he had not felt since childhood stirred within him. Milan recalled the time when he felt God's protective hand guiding and blessing him. But the doubts of his teenage years strove against this new hope, bringing hostile memories of the priest's hypocrisy and the senseless bloodshed of war. Sighing, Milan walked on with Anka at his side. They completed their walk in silence, a somber, contemplative pair amid festive townspeople out to enjoy the evening.

* * * * *

Milan and Anka were drawn to each other for different reasons. He was attracted by her competence at the pharmacy, and even though he was very suspicious of organized religion, he admired her steadfast faith in God. He also felt like he had finally found someone in whom he could confide and share his struggles and doubts. His mother was always either exhausted, drunk, or both; his sisters were too young to be burdened by such heavy troubles; and he was alienated, more or less, from the rest of society. For some time now, Milan had been very much alone. In Anka, he had finally found a listening ear and a sympathetic heart.

Anka, on the other hand, was drawn to Milan by a caring instinct. She could see that he was a deeply damaged individual and that his case was hopeless without the aid of a close friend. Her experience in caring for her younger siblings and for the sick people who came to her pharmacy had made her into a profoundly compassionate woman. Anka knew that Milan had many good qualities and great potential though he was sadly limited by the dark depression that had resulted from his time in the war. And closer to her heart than the rosary and crucifix that she always wore was the conviction that God could change people and work the miracle of restoration in their lives. She resolved to help Milan and prayed that someday he would find help from their heavenly Father.

Leaving home

Stomping the March slush from his shoes, Milan walked into his home. His mother stood by the stove with a cigarette in hand and greeted him warmly.

"So, you're finally back. Sit down, close here by the stove, and warm up. You must be tired and cold from having worked so long and from taking the train back in the dark."

"It's fine," Milan said as he took off his shoes and coat. "I'm just happy to have work." He sat down with a little groan, stretched out his back, and scanned the room.

"Where's Anka?" he asked.

"Oh, her," Vida waved her cigarette dismissively. "She's resting in the back room. I told her it would be nice if she waited for you to return, but I guess she couldn't manage even that. But don't worry, son. Your mother is cooking your favorite, bean soup."

Milan smiled absently and fought the urge to have a cigarette. Since they had gotten married a year or so earlier, Anka had tried to convince him to quit smoking, or at least cut down drastically. But at home, the temptation was great because Vida kept the little area constantly full of smoke.

She tried to engage him on several topics, but his answers were short and vague. Finally, he could stand it no longer and went to the back room. Anka was lying awake on the bed in the dark. They greeted each other, and from the tremor in her voice, he could tell she had been crying.

"What's wrong?" he asked her.

"Oh, it's nothing."

"No, really, tell me. I need to know. Why have you been crying?"

Anka sat up on the bed with some effort. She was more than halfway into her pregnancy, and her movements were starting to be more and more restricted.

"I'm sorry," she whispered. "I know that I should be grateful for living here for free, and I know how much you love your mother, but I can't take it anymore. Today while she was at work, I cleaned the whole house. I scrubbed the floors, did the laundry and dishes, and took out the trash. When she returned, it was like I had done something wrong. She purposefully kept her muddy shoes on, threw her soaked cloak on the fresh linen on the bed, and is using one of the cups I washed as an ashtray! I swear she does it just to spite me."

Instinctively, Milan opened his mouth to protest. Despite all her faults, Vida was still his mother, and he tolerated no disrespect toward her. But her voice came from the front room and cut him off.

"Come get your dinner! I made it the way you like it, something Anka should learn if she plans to try to take care of you. Oh, and tell her to grab a pail and bring me a bucket of water from the well."

And just like that, something in Milan changed. Taking Anka by the hand, he walked back into the front room and went up to his mother.

"We're leaving," he said, quietly but clearly.

"What?" Vida's cigarette fell from her mouth in her astonishment.

"Thank you for letting us stay here for so long, but the time has come for us to find our own place. It is already so cramped with the two of us in addition to you and the girls, and now with a baby on the way, there will be even less room."

"But—" started Vida.

Milan held up his hand. "I am sorry, Mother, but we really have to go. I know an apartment that is available right now. I have been thinking about this for some time, but tonight I realized that it must happen."

Anka started to collect various items of clothing and put them into the one bag they owned. As the realization of her son's leaving slowly dawned on Vida, anger flared in her eyes. But only for a moment, then it died, leaving only embers of sadness.

"I suppose you must. It is probably for the best. May God bless you, my son." She had no words for Anka.

Holding their possessions—the bag of clothes and a washbasin—Milan and Anka left his childhood home and set out to find a new one of their own.

* * * * *

Leaving his childhood home was a tremendous step in Milan's life. To start his journey of recovery with Anka by his side, he had to free himself of the overbearing, and sometimes toxic, presence of his mother. Only then could he move toward establishing a family and finding reconciliation with God. The environment of his childhood home was chaotic and disorderly, a poor place to raise children and aspire to live a clean, godly life. A new home would mean a fresh start. And though it seemed at the time as if he were abandoning his mother to her degradation, time would prove that this necessary, albeit painful, step would eventually bring Milan to a condition in which he would have the strength and resources to help his mother change her lifestyle and find God.

The turning point

Milan sat and stared through the window. Outside, Anka was busy in the garden, tending the fresh green shoots that were budding under the warming influence of spring. Though her still-youthful face bore the first etches of worry and pain after losing their baby, she kept herself active and occupied by tending to the new life bursting from the fertile soil. But Milan sat idle, his hands cradled listlessly in his lap. The shadow cast over him by the war had darkened, deepening his former restless turmoil into a profoundly hopeless apathy.

There was a knock on the door, but he didn't stir. Instead, he waited until the knocks become loud enough to summon Anka from the garden. Wiping her hands on her apron and suppressing her annoyance at her husband, Anka opened the door and greeted their visitor. It was Lena, a pleasant, middle-aged woman bearing a cloth-covered basket in one hand and a book bag in the other.

"Hello, Anka," she said in greeting. "I am so happy to see you again. Here are some doughnuts that I pulled out of the oven right before coming here. Hello, nephew."

Anka thanked her and put the basket of sugary doughnuts on the table. Milan grunted in the direction of his aunt but kept his eyes fixed vacantly on the window. The women sat down on the sofa at the far end of the room and exchanged pleasantries.

"The garden looks nice," Lena remarked, gazing through the same window on which Milan was fixated. "You seem to have settled down quite well."

"Thank you," Anka replied. A strain of sadness crept into her voice. "I spend as much time as I can out there. The fresh air and hard work clear my mind, though they cannot lift my spirits."

"There, there," Lena patted her hand. "These things happen very often with firstborns. And while it is important to grieve, it is also important to remember that life continually springs anew. Just look at those beautiful yellow flowers that are blooming in your garden!"

Anka wiped away a tear and bravely attempted to smile. To buy some time to compose herself, she went to the kitchen and brought back some tea to go with Lena's doughnuts. Anka offered some to Milan, but he shook his head gloomily. The women helped themselves and savored the sweetness.

"Is he always like this?" Lena asked, her voice lowered discreetly.

"Only on Sundays," Anka answered. "On working days, he is too exhausted to do anything other than eat and collapse into bed."

"Well, thank God for that welding job."

"Yes," agreed Anka, "thank God."

Lena took several pamphlets and a large, worn Bible out of the book bag. The two women bowed their heads for a short prayer, but Milan was unmoved—only a hint of a frown betrayed his foul mood.

"Today, I thought we'd spend some time in the third chapter of the Gospel of John," Lena said, starting their Bible study. "It is one of the most famous chapters in the Bible, and it contains the most profound verse of all."

Anka listened attentively, reverentially, while Lena spoke. Milan hunched his shoulders and concentrated on the windowpane.

"The chapter begins with a meeting between Jesus and Nicodemus. Nicodemus was a Pharisee who believed in Christ but came to Him at night lest his reputation should suffer. This is what Jesus told him: 'Very truly I tell you, no one can see the kingdom of God unless they are born again' (John 3:3). This puzzled Nicodemus because he could not understand how someone who had already been born could be born again. He did not understand that Jesus was speaking metaphorically. Then Jesus explained: 'Very truly I tell you, no one can enter the kingdom of God unless they are born of water and the Spirit' " (verse 5).

On the other side of the room, unbeknownst to the women, Milan was listening to Lena's words. A battle raged in his heart. On one side were all his old prejudices against religion, drenched in anger and despair and allied with the tremendous guilt he felt for participating in the brutal butchery of the war. On the other side was a faint new hope—a flicker of the flame lit in his childhood by the miracle near the Ukrina River and now rekindled by the faith of his wife. Which side would prevail?

Lena continued, "Christ's explanation only confused Nicodemus more. So, Jesus made things plain to him with the most wonderful verse in the Bible. He explained to Nicodemus that rebirth through baptism and in the Spirit was a sign of accepting the great gift of salvation that God granted us through the sacrifice of his Son. Jesus said, 'For God so loved the world that he gave his one and only Son, that whoever believes in him shall not perish but have eternal life' " (verse 16).

Milan sat up straight and paid close attention. Anka gasped and asked, "Can it really be? Can God really forgive people and save them despite all the terrible things they have done? I was taught in church that God judged and punished us. That was my main motivation to be religious."

"Why don't you see for yourself?" Lena carefully passed the Bible over to her. "There, in verse seventeen. Go ahead, read it."

" 'For God did not send his Son into the world to condemn the world, but to save the world through him.' "

"So, you see," Lena concluded, "God can save anyone in the whole world."

"What was that? What did you say?" Milan abruptly broke in, but his voice was still low from the long silence he had subjected himself to.

Not noticing him, Lena and Anka continued talking.

"What did you say?" Milan spoke up, seizing their attention. "Can God really save the worst sinners? What about priests who curse? What about soldiers who kill and destroy?"

Unflinching, Lena stared straight at him.

"Yes," she said. "God can save anyone. Even someone like you."

His heart on fire, Milan leaped up, grabbed his chair, and bounded over to their side of the room to join them in the Bible study.

* * * * *

From that moment on, Milan was an avid student of God's Word, and his life began the slow, painful process of spiritual transformation. It would be a long, arduous journey, but now that he was set on learning more about God, there was no turning back from the path of faith.

Every weekend, Lena spent hours with Anka and Milan, and together they delved deeper into the key stories contained in the Bible. They learned of the wonders of Creation and the blessed gift of the Sabbath day. They heard of Lucifer's rebellion and the tragic fall of humanity. They were amazed by the plan of salvation and the transference of that wondrous hope through the patriarchs, judges, kings, and prophets—all the way to the coming of the promised Messiah, Jesus Christ. They rejoiced in God's offer of forgiveness and in Christ's ultimate victory on the cross over sin and death. And their grief at the death of their firstborn child was assuaged by the hope in the second coming of Christ and the promise of life everlasting.

Through the powerful testimony of the Word of God and under the guiding influence of His Spirit, Lena led the two new believers toward a new life in Christ.

Farewell to an old habit

Deep in sleep, Anka was roused yet again by an all-too-familiar commotion. Through sleep-laden eyes, she peered in the dimness of a low-lit lamp at the shape beside her. Milan was thrashing—his arms wrapped in bedsheets—and groaning in agony. Sweat ran down his face as he ground his teeth in terror. Anka reached out and shook him awake. Milan's eyes snapped open, and he stared right at her. Though he was wide awake, Milan seemed to be far away, caught in a battle that had ended long ago, fighting enemies long dead. Anka reached out to hold him and offer him comfort, but Milan was already out of bed and staggering toward the living room. She followed him and caught him in the act of lighting a cigarette.

"Milan! What are you doing?" Anka exclaimed.

"Be quiet," he said crossly. "Don't wake up the baby."

"The baby!" Anka was furious. "Is that what you are concerned about? Our new baby? Is that why you are about to fill our home with poisonous fumes?"

Milan put down the poised match and hung his head in shame.

"I was going to go outside," he said, shifting his feet. "I had a terrible dream. It was about the war. I was in a field full of blood, and there were bodies everywhere."

His voice trailed off as the horror of the dream returned.

"I am sorry." Anka's voice was gentler. "I really am. I know it is hard for you to deal with what you went through in the past. But that is no excuse to ruin your health and put your family at risk from secondhand smoke. You know better than that. You are a stronger man than that."

"No, I am not." Milan's face was dark in the shadows. "But you can help me. Here, take this."

He held out his pack to her.

"Hide it someplace where I can't find it."

"Sure, I can do that." Anka crossed her arms. "Just like I have, what, a dozen, two dozen, times before?"

Milan said nothing. The cigarette pack remained in his outstretched hand, suspended in the space between the two young believers.

"Or," continued Anka, "you could get rid of them yourself."

Milan raised his face and gazed at his wife. A struggle had started within him. Though he was silent, his whole being pled with Anka to keep speaking, to say something that would give him the strength to break free from this vile old habit and face the horrors of the past without the crutch of nicotine.

"Sit down," Anka directed him. She lit another lamp on the coffee table and opened a New Testament that Lena had given them.

"Do you remember the Bible study we had a couple of weeks ago, the one about the apostle Paul's letter to the Corinthians?"

"Yes, I think so," a subdued Milan replied.

Anka read out loud, "Do you not know that your bodies are temples of the Holy Spirit, who is in you, whom you have received from God? You are not your own; you were bought at a price. Therefore honor God with your bodies" (1 Corinthians 6:19, 20).

A stern look came over Milan's face. Setting his jaw in grim determination, he crushed the pack of cigarettes in his fist and strode out the back door. Under the eye of a full, luminous moon, he tossed the broken cigarettes into the garbage pit at the far end of the garden.

Back inside, he found Anka feeding the baby. Milan went to them and put his arms around mother and child.

"It is done," he murmured. "Now, with God's grace, I am free of this harmful substance."

"Praise God," Anka said and, bowing her head, led the little family in a prayer of thanksgiving.

* * * * *

Quitting smoking was just one of the many changes that Milan went through during his gradual conversion. Other areas of his life had to be transformed through the power of God before he could become a true believer and join the church.

With the help of Lena and Anka and under the guidance of the Holy Spirit, Milan learned to live a happier and healthier life. His diet, his behavior, and even his thoughts all had to undergo a radical change. All his troubles had stemmed from a lack of direction, from a false point of view that did not acknowledge God's grace and power.

But as he slowly learned to rely on the Lord and seek divine guidance through prayer and a diligent study of His Word, his lifestyle began to conform to the Edenic principles God had instituted at Creation for the benefit of humankind. The coming years would hold many tribulations for the new believers. To be able to rise to the challenges ahead, it was very important for Milan to be sound in both body and mind. There was no way to erase the past, but by depending on God and conforming to His will, Milan would repent and turn the other way to bravely face future trials with God's help.

A light in the dark

The night was pitch black. Hidden in a hollow covered by brambles, Milan, Anka, and Pastor Radovan had crouched for hours as they waited for complete darkness. Finally, it was dark enough, and the pastor took them by the hand and whispered that the time had come. Milan did not let go of his hand.

"Thank you," whispered Milan.

“Please don’t mention it,” the pastor replied. “It is an honor to baptize the second and third Adventist believers in Derventa.”

“But you have traveled so far,” Milan insisted. “All the way from Banja Luka just for the two of us. How can we ever repay you?”

“God will see to my reward, brother,” the pastor said. He squeezed Milan’s hand. “Anyway, getting to be the one who admits you into the fold is reward enough for me!”

The three of them scrambled out of the hollow and stumbled blindly through the bushes toward the riverbank. They slid down the bank and splashed into the shallow water. A few stars peeped through the draped branches of surrounding willow trees, but this faint light only served to accentuate the darkness. Milan and Anka stood side by side as Pastor Radovan recited the questions that are asked of all those who choose to be members of the Seventh-day Adventist Church.

“Do you believe in God the Father, in His Son Jesus Christ, and in the Holy Spirit?”

With one voice, Milan and Anka responded, “I do.”

The pastor and the two new believers moved on down the list until they came to the very last vow.

“Do you desire to be a member of this local assembly of the world church?”

“I do,” they replied.

The pastor prayed and then extended his hands toward them. Anka went first—the one to introduce the truth to Milan through her Bible studies with Lena. The pastor wasted no time, and before they knew it, Milan and Anka were back on the riverbank, drenched from head to toe in the cold water and shivering in the night chill. But within them, a holy glow pulsed and spread, filling them with an irrepressible warmth and a blessed assurance. God’s presence had come on them in the form of His promised Spirit. That night they completed the first stage of the journey that had started when they began studying God’s Word with Lena. Now they were part of the great family of God!

* * * * *

Their baptism, that blessed moment of eternal significance, had to take place under cover of darkness because of the political situation.

In the first years after the Second World War, when the nation was still young and ideological zeal was at its fever pitch, any viewpoint that was not fully aligned with that of the atheistic ruling party was viewed with great suspicion and could result in serious consequences. The Adventist church faced hostilities, and several of its leaders were imprisoned. With time, this would change.

But in the days when Milan and Anka were converted, it was very dangerous to openly join a church, especially one with ties to the West. Atheism had become an integral part of the official ideology of the land, and though the traditional Christian and Muslim religions were tolerated, pledging allegiance to what was viewed as a new, foreign faith was unacceptable. Church meetings occurred unofficially in members' homes, with two or three believers gathered around a shared Bible and softly singing songs of faith.

But this did not discourage those early Adventist believers. Drawing on New Testament accounts of similar humble beginnings during the time of the missionary exploits of Paul, Peter, and others, they persevered through hardships and worshiped God in private. Though Milan and Anka were forced to accept Christ as their personal Savior and Friend in secret, their lives would be a public testimony to His saving and transformative power. In the darkness of night, two new lights began to shine brightly!

CHAPTER FIVE

TESTS AND TRIUMPHS

I was pushed back and about to fall,
but the Lord *helped me.*
The Lord *is my strength and my defense;*
he has become my salvation.

Shouts of joy and victory
resound in the tents of the righteous:
"The Lord*'s right hand has done mighty things!*
The Lord*'s right hand is lifted high;*
the Lord*'s right hand has done mighty things!"*
I will not die but live,
and will proclaim what the Lord *has done.*

—Psalm 118:13–17

Taking a stand for the Sabbath

The train moved slowly, chugging along through the predawn mists rising from dew-drenched fields and overflowing the willow-crowded riverbank. Roosters called out from farms nearby; their sound pierced through the train's clamor. Milan sat on a wooden bench, too preoccupied with his thoughts to notice the glorious, golden start of the day in the east before him.

His mind shifted between the immediate future and the barely gone past. He tried to concentrate on the former, but the latter kept breaking in and disrupting his thoughts. Milan tightened his grip on the lunch box filled by Anka with yesterday's leftovers. He pictured himself standing in front of his boss and mentally practiced the words he had resolved to say: "I am sorry, sir, but I must inform you that I cannot work." That was as far as he would get before the other memory broke in. The oppressive dread of that moment returned first, and then the images followed, rushing back to his mind.

In a courtroom, the judge was talking to both Milan and Anka. "I am letting you off easy," he said, "because of comrade Milan's bravery in the war. Others would not have fared so well."

Panic rose in them. It was no small matter to be called in for suspicious behavior. There had been many disappearances recently, most for transgressions far lighter than theirs. And how did the authorities find out about their midnight baptism, anyway? Someone must have been spying and reported them. It didn't feel good to know they were under surveillance.

"What were you thinking, joining an organization with ties to the West? A group that is not sanctioned by the Party! This is subversive behavior. You are not to spread any of this propaganda, nor are you to hold any religious meetings."

The judge glowered at them. They kept their faces expressionless.

"Let this be a warning to you: no more of this religious nonsense. Keep away from unauthorized sects and do your work to further the revolution. I don't want to hear of any more disturbances from you two!"

Back in the train, Milan shook his head clear of the memory. The fresh light of a new day had crept into the sky, and the broad Sava River stretched away on either side as the train clanged over the bridge connecting Bosnia to Croatia. Bowing his head, Milan asked God to give him the strength he needed for the task that lay ahead of him.

"Father God," he prayed, "protect Your humble servant in this moment of trial. I am afraid of the consequences. I do not want to lose my job. My family is growing, and I must provide for them. But I know that what is most important is to faithfully serve Your will and keep Your commandments. I leave the rest in Your hands. Amen."

A few minutes later, the train arrived at the huge factory. Milan, along with hundreds of other workers, hurried inside, joining thousands more for their daily labor under towering smokestacks. Instead of heading to his workstation, Milan directed his steps to his foreman's office.

There, the foreman greeted Milan warmly. He highly esteemed Milan because of his hard work and his skill as a welder. But this only made it harder for Milan to do what he knew he must. How would his boss take this request? Would he see it as a demand? Would he take it as a challenge? Pushing back his fears and the memory of the judge's warning, Milan boldly spoke out.

"I am sorry, comrade, but I must inform you that I cannot work on Saturdays anymore."

The foreman gave him a puzzled look.

"Why, Milan," he asked, "what does this mean? Do you want an extra day off your workweek while everyone else keeps the same hours?"

"No," replied Milan. "Please let me explain."

The foreman nodded.

"I only wish to have one free day a week, as we all do. But I would like that day to be Saturday instead of Sunday."

"I see. That is very strange. Is there a reason for this request?"

"Yes. Saturday is the Lord's Day, the Sabbath, which He blessed at the end of the first week of Creation. The Bible tells us that if we are to worship God properly and keep His commandments, we must honor His Sabbath."

"Hmm," the foreman mused. "I have never heard of Saturday being the holy day. But what do I know about such things? They are your beliefs, not mine. As far as I am concerned, as long as the work gets finished, what difference does it make which day you take off? But I am not the final authority on such matters. Let me go talk to my boss and see what he says."

The foreman disappeared into the office behind his to talk to the regional manager. The minutes trickled by as Milan remained standing, full of hope that was mingled with fear. To help pass the time and to ease his anxiety, he repeated his prayer to God. When he finished, he repeated it again. And again, until his heart was filled with the providential peace of faith.

The foreman returned and sat down with a wry smile.

"Well, it looks like you will get to keep your Sabbath. However, the boss isn't happy about this, and he says that he will dock you a day's worth of wages for every Saturday you miss, even though you have to come to work on Sunday to make up for it. But you aren't getting fired, which is what would have happened if I didn't mention your excellent work as a welder and your heroic deeds in the war. Now, comrade Milan, get to your workstation!"

With a light head and giddy steps, Milan left the office. *I did it!* he thought. *I can keep the Sabbath and my job as well! No—I didn't do it. It was God! He was the one who worked this miracle.*

Bowing his head, Milan humbly offered Him a prayer of thanks.

* * * * *

Keeping the Sabbath, a central tenet of his new faith, would become a source of both divine protection and secular persecution for Milan. On the one hand, it was a temporal refuge, a special time set aside for prayer, praise, and the study of God's Word in the fellowship of other believers. Within its sacred bounds, Milan found divine protection from the troubles of the world. On the other hand, his strict observance of the seventh-day Sabbath brought him into conflict with many intolerant people. On the surface was the dominating, atheistic ideology of the day that scorned such spiritual devotion. And underneath lurked the old, dogmatic opposition of the traditional Christian religions to a day of worship other than Sunday.

Milan was viewed in public as an ignorant fanatic and in private as a troublemaking heretic. This brought him into conflict with many people and caused a succession of persecutions. But some were intrigued by his zealous faith in such godless times and touched by his devotion. Thus, through his stand for the Sabbath, Milan began to witness to those of his neighbors who were receptive and draw them closer to Christ.

Debate by a deathbed

In a room dimly lit by a few rays of sun streaming in around drawn curtains, Milan sat beside the bed in which Lena lay. Her eyes were shut, and she was still except for the labored breaths that heaved the mound of blankets heaped atop her. Her weak and wasted face wore a weariness that no ordinary, temporary rest could remedy. Milan gingerly took her hand in his. It was cold and trembling. On a nearby dresser sat the uneaten meal that Anka prepared for him to bring over. All Lena could manage was a couple of polite mouthfuls. Milan prayed in a low, soft voice, asking God to comfort her in these last moments. When he finished, Lena spoke.

"Thank you, brother Milan. It is very kind of you to visit me. It means so much. I know that God has sent you to me."

"You are welcome," Milan replied, patting the hand he held. "But it is nothing. This is what fellow believers should do for each other. And Anka would have come, too, if it were not for the little ones."

"Yes, bless her," Lena spoke shakily. "The food she prepared is wonderful, as always. I understand why she could not come. Others need looking after."

She smiled faintly at Milan, and, despite the somber mood, he could not help but beam back at her. His family was growing, and it filled him with irrepressible joy.

A couple of heavy thuds sounded on the front door. Lena sighed deeply.

"Oh no," she murmured. "Not again."

Without waiting for admittance, the person outside opened the door and strode in with loud, authoritative steps. He was a large man and filled the room with his bulk. He was dressed in rich black robes, and his hair and beard were long. An ornate gold crucifix gleamed on his chest. Paying Milan no heed, the priest addressed his words to Lena.

"Good afternoon, daughter." The words sounded more like a command than a greeting. He got straight to the point.

"I have come to see if you have decided to listen to reason. Will you recant and renounce this upstart sect that has corrupted your faith in the holy church?"

Lena closed her eyes and shook her head. Her hand tightened around Milan's.

The priest frowned like a storm cloud.

"I see. So you persist in your heresy, despite my repeated efforts. How many times have I visited you since I heard that you were on your deathbed to exhort you to return to the church of our fathers? And for what? You are as hard-hearted as a heathen."

"Excuse me, Father," Milan broke in. "But this is a woman near death. You should be respectful of her beliefs and allow her to depart in peace."

"I know that she is near death!" thundered the priest with flashing eyes. "That is precisely why I am here. Her time is running out."

He turned back to Lena. "Let me warn you again: if you do not recant, there will be no place for you to be buried in the cemetery, just as there will be no place for you in the heavenly kingdom!"

"Why do you say such things?" Milan cried, getting agitated in response to the priest's harsh words. "What gives you the right to deny her the basic rights of the deceased?"

"She has lost her faith! As have you!"

"All we have done is read the Bible and followed God's Word. Is that losing faith?"

"Reading the Bible!" the priest raged. "It is not for you to read and interpret holy Scripture. You should humble yourself and follow the tradition of your forefathers."

Milan composed himself and spoke calmly. "If I have to choose between the traditions of our forefathers and the words of Christ, I choose Christ."

"I am finished here. There is no use in speaking to stones. You have chosen your doom." Glaring, the priest turned to leave.

"You have changed your faith," he shot a parting volley.

"No," Milan replied, still holding Lena's frail hand. "My faith has changed me."

* * * * *

The priest was not the only one in town who did not accept Milan's conversion. Many others were skeptical and critical of his newfound faith and the new Adventist church in Derventa.

In those early years of his belief, Milan would often be accosted by neighbors upon returning from work in the evening. Though he would be bone-weary from the long hours of welding, he always stopped to answer their questions and accusations, doing his best to explain to them the biblical foundations and positive personal effects of his faith. Many doubted his words.

"Look at you, acting holy," they scoffed. "You can't fool us. We know you. You curse, you never go to church, you smoke, and you are short-tempered."

"Do you see me doing those things now?" Milan would retort. "Do not judge my faith by my past, but by the changes it is making in me today."

Some would stop and think about this, but many would close their eyes to the truth of Milan's words. It would take some time until the profound changes manifested in his character would force even the most cynical to acknowledge that he had undergone a true transformation that could have been bestowed only by the grace of God. Until then, Milan would have to face some of the harshest harassment and persecution of his Christian life.

Two funerals

"Father, please, have mercy. Where else can we bury her? She cannot go to the Jewish cemetery, the Muslim cemetery, or the Catholic cemetery. Her background is Orthodox. She belongs here even if she found a new faith. Please reconsider."

The priest smiled as he listened to these words. He leaned back in his chair and rubbed his hands together, clearly relishing the moment. His smile widened.

"Well, well," he said. "So you have finally decided to come to church. And it seems that Lena wants to return, too, eh?"

Milan said nothing. The priest's smile stayed pasted on his face though his voice hardened underneath.

"Do you remember what I told you only a week ago? Did I not warn you? Then, there was still time for her. Now it is too late. There is no room for her here among those of the true faith. She chose this, and you supported her in her incorrigible heresy. Now you must reap what you have sown."

"Please, do not do this. All I am asking for is a little spot somewhere out of the way where we can bury her in peace. She is still a child of God, like me and like you, too."

"Do not compare yourselves to me!" The priest's face darkened with anger. "And stop wasting my time with these impertinent demands. She abandoned the church and joined a heretical sect. She is an outcast, in death as in life. If the gates of heaven are closed to her, how will the gates of the church's cemetery admit her?"

"Father, I beg you."

"No! Begone! She will never be buried here. Let her corpse rot like that of all sectarians."

His finger pointed to the door. The discussion was over.

Milan walked out of the church and headed straight for the mayor's office. There, the secretary hastily ushered him in ahead of a line of waiting people. The mayor rose from his seat to greet him. After a few salutatory sentences, Milan shared his problem.

"I need your help, comrade. There is a great injustice that is being committed."

The mayor cocked his head to the side.

"Tell me," Milan spoke determinedly with squared shoulders, "why did we fight in that horrible war? For what did we sacrifice our brothers and our youth? Was it not for a new, free society in which ordinary citizens are valued and respected? Was it not for equality and fraternity that we overthrew the old order and expelled the invaders?"

"Indeed, that is precisely why," concurred the mayor.

"Then why is it that my good aunt Lena, an honest, hardworking, patriotic citizen, is denied a decent burial now that she has passed away? What crime has she committed that her body cannot be laid to rest where her ancestors have been buried?"

"Go on," urged the mayor. "Explain this to me fully."

"It is the Orthodox priest. He says that she cannot be buried in the church cemetery because she changed her faith. And yet he buries atheistic Party members there every week! If their Orthodox background qualifies them for the cemetery, why doesn't Lena's?"

"You are absolutely right," agreed the mayor. "This is an injustice, and I will personally see to it that your friend is given a proper burial where she belongs. Do not worry; all will be taken care of. Now go, get her body ready and conduct your services. Just tell me when the funeral will take place, and I will deal with the priest."

The next day, a very strange scene unfolded in the Orthodox cemetery. It just so happened that another funeral was scheduled to take place at the exact time that Lena was to be buried. The other funeral was for a wealthy merchant, and scores of people, dressed in fine suits and rich furs, showed up to see his gilded casket interred. His marble tombstone was carved with an impressive list of achievements, and a sea of garish flowers surrounded the grave.

Lena's coffin was made of the cheapest wood, and a wooden cross was the sole marker of her resting place. A handful of her brothers and sisters in Christ gathered in a humble corner of the cemetery reserved for the less illustrious members of society. At the gate of the cemetery, two stern policemen stood. The mayor had kept his promise.

The rich man's funeral began. The priest chanted in an ancient language that no one fully understood and swayed the censer emitting the sickly sweet–smelling incense. The crowd responded instinctively, mechanically joining in the chant at the appropriate places, but their hearts were not truly involved in the service.

At the other end of the cemetery, the small group of believers began to sing, faintly at first but then with a growing vigor born of profound conviction. "In the sweet by and by, we shall meet on that beautiful shore."[1]

By the rich man's grave, heads began to turn in the direction of Lena's funeral.

Pastor Radovan, who had traveled all the way from Banja Luka again, just as he did for Milan and Anka's baptism, began to speak in a language understood by and accessible to all. His strong, clear voice carried over the crumbling tombstones and mossy graves, rising above the mindless drone of the priest's chant.

"Today we are gathered, dear brothers and sisters, not in sadness but in joy. For though our beloved Lena is gone from us, we know that she is only sleeping in Christ and that someday we will see her again!"

A couple of well-dressed figures detached themselves from the crowd around the rich man's burial and furtively made their way to Lena's graveside. The pastor continued speaking.

"Just like our lives, our deaths are only temporary. Sister Lena knew this, and now she sleeps in the assurance that someday she will awaken and arise to meet her Redeemer returning in angelic clouds of glory. For Jesus Himself said, 'I am the resurrection and the life. The one who believes in me will live, even though they die' " (John 11:25).

As the pastor kept speaking, sharing, and comforting his flock with words full of wisdom and hope, a slow but steady flow of people streamed from the rich man's funeral to Lena's side of the cemetery. By the time the pastor concluded, more people were gathered around Lena's grave than the merchant's. The newcomers listened attentively, curious to hear for the first time in their lives a sermon founded firmly on the Word of God. Tears ran down the faces of Milan and his fellow believers—tears of joy, sprung by witnessing the awesome miracle wrought by God through Lena's funeral. God had not only provided a way through the mayor to allow Lena to be buried properly but also began the work of salvation in the cold and lifeless hearts of the jaded, disinterested wealthy. Truly, two miracles had taken place as the result of the death of a believer. Praise God!

* * * * *

A recurring theme of the persecutions Milan had to face as a new believer was that God would always find a way to turn a hardship into a blessing, whether the transformation came immediately or gradually. What had started as an impossible situation, with the priest refusing to relent and taking a perverse delight in Milan's predicament, had miraculously turned into a public display of God's power. Through the mayoral support of the rights of the fledgling Adventist flock, the townspeople could see that this was a legitimate group of believers, a group that deserved to be treated with decency and respect. And through the wondrous work of the Holy Spirit, which drew so many from the priest's service by the grave of the rich man, the community could see the value and the earnest truth of the Adventist pastor's message. Thus, good came out of bad.

Bookselling

Milan walked up a low hill, the gravel crunching under his feet. He climbed with slow, though determined, steps. *What will I find in the house at the top of the hill?* he mused. *Will it be a receptive person with a heart open to God's message of hope? Or will it be a hostile person, entrenched in atheism or violently drunk?* Praying to God for support, Milan crested the hill and walked through the courtyard between pecking chickens and barking dogs. The commotion roused the inhabitants of the house, and before Milan could knock on the door, it opened. He came to an abrupt standstill, the color draining from his face. He didn't know what to say.

Standing in front of him was a well-dressed man. His expensive tie, tailored suit, and gleaming shoes stood out sharply against the farm setting. His face wore the assured, measured look of someone accustomed to holding authority over others. It was the judge who had warned Milan and Anka some years before to keep his faith under wraps. With a keen glance, the judge took in the bag of religious books and pamphlets slung over Milan's shoulder and instantly realized what he was up to.

"So," he said, placing his hands on his hips, "you did not take my warning seriously. Instead, you are spreading your religious doctrines with those books." The judge shook his head in disbelief.

Milan blinked and rallied, summoning all his strength to face this man of power and consequence. Milan's freedom and the survival of his family, who depended upon him for support, were on the line.

"I do not mean any disrespect," he said. "But my God and my faith mean everything to me. They have saved my life and are transforming me into a better person. And if I am to be true to them, I must spread the gospel as all true believers are called to do. I cannot contain the good news within me and not share it with everyone I meet."

The judge considered Milan's bold words. He rubbed his chin thoughtfully. "And those books?" he inquired."What do they have to do with your convictions?"

"There is nothing wrong with these books," said Milan. "They are full of truths about God's love for us and how we can live our lives to the fullest. They can only help, and not harm, those who choose to read them."

"Hmm." The judge looked at the bulging bag more closely. "That's a lot of books. Are you planning on selling all of them? What will you do with all that money?"

"The money that I make from selling these books will be returned to the publishers to cover the printing costs so that more books can be made. And instead of taking my allotted percentage of the sales, I give two of every ten books for free to those who cannot afford them."

The judge said nothing to this, clearly taken aback by Milan's zeal and selflessness.

"See for yourself," Milan entreated. "I have many books here for many kinds of people. Books written in Cyrillic for those of Orthodox background. Books written in Latin for those of Catholic background. And books without the symbol of the cross on their covers for our atheist and Muslim neighbors who might take offense. There is nothing harmful or offensive about these books. They are meant to spread hope to all."

Milan set down the heavy bag and opened it to show the judge the books, but before he could approach, the door swung open, and a little girl ran out. She darted straight to the book bag and grabbed a blue book with a picture of a group of people staring at the heavens with glory radiating from their upturned faces. The title of the book was *Christ's Believers Through the Ages.*

"Daddy, Daddy," she cried, "please get this one for me."

Milan was puzzled. So was the judge.

"Why do you want this book?" he asked his daughter. "It looks like you recognize it."

"I do," she said happily, nodding her head and shaking her yellow curls. "Teacher always reads it to us in class. It is full of such wonderful stories. It is my favorite! Please get it for me, Daddy."

The judge scratched his head. Milan waited to see how the situation would resolve itself.

"Go ask your mother for money," the judge told her. "If she will pay for it, you can have it."

The girl dashed back into the house. Moments later, she reappeared and thrust a bill into the hand of a very startled Milan and, grabbing the book, disappeared back into the house. The two men stood there, staring at each other over the opened bag of books.

The judge broke the silence, speaking slowly and thoughtfully. "This is very strange. I do not understand how such books, religious ones, could have been read to my daughter in a public school."

But Milan knew the answer. God had worked a miracle and found a way to reach this man through his daughter!

"There must be something to these books," the judge continued, "if my daughter was affected so profoundly by them. Do you have any that might be of interest to me? I am here on a visit out of town and have brought my family to stay with my mother. There isn't much to do here in the countryside, and it would be good to have something to read."

Milan called down the hill, and Stefan, his youngest son of a growing family, ran up the hill with a second bag of books. After browsing through both bags, the judge selected half a dozen and paid handsomely for them. Then he bowed in farewell to Milan.

As Milan and his son walked away, their feet felt like they had wings. What an incredible turnaround! What had seemed to be a disastrously coincidental encounter with a top official who had previously warned Milan to keep his faith to himself had turned out to be the sale of the day. Truly, this strange encounter had been no accident, no strange coincidence, but the providential work of the hand of God, helping those who labor to spread His Word.

* * * * *

Besides leading an upright daily life, selling books was one of the main ways in which Milan witnessed. With heavy bags hung on his bike and one of his sons to help him, Milan would travel all over town and into the countryside, selling these books of hope and spreading God's Word. Though the weather and sometimes the people they encountered could be harsh, Milan persevered and continued faithfully in this ministry. And God blessed not only those who bought the books and accepted His message but also Milan, who sold the books and thereby grew in faith. The story of the judge and his daughter dramatically illustrates the power of God in spreading His Word.

---

1. Sanford Fillmore Bennett, "In the Sweet By and By," 1868, public domain.

CHAPTER SIX

MORE TESTS AND TRIUMPHS

"You have heard that it was said,
'Love your neighbor and hate your enemy.'
But I tell you, love your enemies and pray for those who persecute you,
that you may be children of your Father in heaven.
He causes his sun to rise on the evil and the good,
and sends rain on the righteous and the unrighteous.
If you love those who love you, what reward will you get?
Are not even the tax collectors doing that?
And if you greet only your own people,
what are you doing more than others?
Do not even pagans do that?
Be perfect, therefore, as your heavenly Father is perfect."
—Matthew 5:43–48

Christmas without oranges

"Look at this fellow, acting saintly, as if he were better than the rest of us. What are you reading, Milan? The Bible? Who reads such an obsolete book nowadays? Ha ha ha!"

The loud, rude words came from the mouth of Milan's new supervisor. Ever since he had arrived at the factory, he had made trouble for Milan. The supervisor had threatened to fire him and to lower his already reduced salary, and he openly mocked Milan when he witnessed to his coworkers during the lunch hour. Now the supervisor harassed Milan while he read the Bible during a short break. With his mind resolutely focused on the Word, Milan strove to ignore the taunts and rise above the resentment that began to grow in his heart.

Milan kept reading and praying silently. He refused to engage this man who was looking for trouble. Reading God's Word provided him with spiritual nourishment, which he needed as much as physical food. Finding no response in Milan, the supervisor turned to the workers who closely observed the situation.

"There is no God," he brazenly proclaimed. "This is the twentieth century. Human thinkers have shown us that all this is superstitious stuff."

Turning toward Milan, he continued to challenge him, "Can your God create a rock so heavy that He cannot lift it?"

A few of the workers nodded their heads in agreement. Most just stood and stared. Milan answered, "I believe He can. He created us human beings and gave us free will, but many do not care about Him. When you act like this, you are that rock!"

"I don't know about you, comrades," the supervisor pressed on, ignoring Milan's clever rebuff, "but I don't need outdated and debunked traditions. Do you know who is my god?"

With an arrogant smile, he drew his wallet out of his back pocket. Waving it in the air, he said, "This is my god. When it is full of bills, I can feel it. It is real. I can count on it. And do you know who puts those bills there? I do!"

The supervisor looked down at Milan with contempt.

"Maybe if you spent less time reading that outdated book and more time making money, you would have a wallet worth worshiping," he snarled, striding arrogantly away.

Some months later, Milan surprised Anka by returning home from work early. His face was ashen, and his hands were trembling.

"What's wrong, Milan?" she asked as she pulled a chair out for him and poured him a cup of tea.

Milan took a few sips of the soothing chamomile and drew in a heavy breath.

"Thank God, Anka! A few hours ago, my life was spared. But I am afraid some of my coworkers were not so fortunate."

Anka, her face grave, sat down at the table with him.

"What happened?"

"You know how today we were supposed to start the welding work on the train? Well, yesterday, the evening crew set up the scaffolding. But they must have worked late and been tired, because they forgot to tighten some of the bolts. This morning, five of us, including my supervisor, climbed the scaffolding to begin work. When we reached the top, the scaffolding collapsed. All four of my coworkers fell to the ground, and the scaffolding and tools fell down on them. Three of them are dead, and the supervisor is badly injured. By the grace of God, I was able to grab a rope that was dangling from the roof. I felt my feet almost touching a live wire below. I do not know how I was not electrocuted."

"God must have saved you," Anka said, putting her steady hand on his trembling one. "Today has been a day of not one miracle but two. Praise the Lord."

"Yes," Milan agreed, "praise Him. For surely today He saved my life."

A week later, it was Christmas day. The numerous children—for Milan and Anka's family had grown—ran excitedly around the house. Delicious smells emanated from the kitchen, but this wasn't the only source of the joyful anticipation of the little ones. On the dining table was a sack of ripe oranges, the traditional gift that each child received for Christmas.

Milan called the children to the table.

"My dear children," he said, "as you know, on Christmas Day, you all receive an orange as a gift. But this Christmas I would like to ask you to make a sacrifice. Only a week ago, God spared my life in a horrific accident. While others were maimed and killed, I walked away unharmed and alive. Today I will take our Christmas present and give it to someone less fortunate than we are. What do you think of this?"

The children enthusiastically gave their support, and Anka beamed at them with motherly pride and appreciation. Taking the hand of Stefan, the youngest, in his left hand, Milan took the bag of oranges in his right hand and left the cheery scene. Together they walked through the snowy streets toward the hospital.

There, in a bare room that was stark compared to the cheerful home they had just left, Milan and Stefan found the supervisor. He was lying on a bed. Both of his legs were amputated above the knee. Milan stood beside him, and the man sensed Milan's presence and opened his eyes.

"Milan," he gasped. "What are you doing here?"

"I have come to wish you a Merry Christmas and to give you a gift from my family. Come, Stefan."

The little boy brought the bag of oranges and put it gently on the bed by the man.

"Thank you," said the supervisor, his eyes round with amazement. "How did you survive the fall?" he asked.

"My God saved me," Milan answered simply. "He cares for me, and He cares for you too. This is the message I came to bring to you today. Will you allow us to pray for you?"

With tears streaming down his face, the supervisor nodded, too moved for words. Together, the three of them joined in prayer to God.

* * * * *

That was a Christmas that Milan's children would never forget. Not only was their father miraculously spared from death a week earlier, but they learned a valuable lesson in forgiveness and gift giving when Milan took the bag of oranges to the man who had previously mocked him.

If God has been so gracious to save my life, Milan reasoned, *how can I not mirror His grace by giving a generous gift to my stricken supervisor?* Milan realized that as a sinner, he did not deserve God's grace. But God had still intervened and protected him. Likewise, the supervisor who had harassed him so ceaselessly did not deserve the gift of oranges, let alone forgiveness.

But those who receive God's grace must respond to His providence by showing grace to their fellow sinners, yes, even to those who are hostile to the faithful. So, Milan forgave his supervisor and gave him the bag of Christmas oranges as a token of God's grace toward all sinners. In the midst of suffering, God's miracle produced another miracle of forgiveness on that Christmas day.

Bullying at school

In the kitchen of their humble home, Anka bent over a large bucket with soapsuds up to her elbows. Next to her, a baby screamed in a cradle, which Anka rocked between washing pieces of clothing. On the other side of the room, a toddler and a five-year-old were playing underneath the dining table. Two big pots were bubbling on the woodstove: one pot full of stew for dinner and the other full of melting snow for the next batch of laundry. Anka paused her work—not to take a break but to dash outside into the winter chill to grab a few more logs to add to the diminishing pile by the stove. Then she returned to the heap of laundry and the crying baby.

The door creaked open, and a slight figure slipped in. Before the figure could sneak away to the bedroom, Anka called, "Pavle, come here."

The boy shuffled over to stand in front of his mother. He hung his head in shame.

"Look at your clothes! Didn't I just wash them the other day? How did you get them so dirty and torn? And what happened to your face? Why is your nose bleeding?"

Pavle shrugged his shoulders. "I tripped and fell into a ditch when I was coming home. I'm sorry."

"Nonsense," Anka said, pulling him closer for a better look. "One of your eyes is black. And there are bruises all over your arms."

She set aside her laundry with a deep sigh and told the other two children to come out from under the table and rock the cradle. Taking the water off the stove, she filled a basin and gave Pavle a bath. Then she dressed him in clean pajamas and gave him some handpicked, home-brewed chamomile tea and a slice of freshly baked bread.

"Now," she said gently. "Tell me what really happened. I don't believe you fell into a ditch. This is what you told me last week and the week before."

The boy hesitated, and then the whole story came rushing out, accompanied by a few tears.

"It all started with my teacher. Every Monday morning, he makes me stand up in front of the class, and he asks me why I didn't come to class on Saturday. I try to explain to him about the Sabbath, but he just makes fun of me and says that school is more important than church. When I show him my finished homework and tell him how I study on Sunday to make up for what I missed, he dismisses me and says that I am unnecessarily complicating things because of a ridiculous belief in God. Most of the other children laugh while this is going on."

Pavle stopped and munched sadly on the snack. Anka stroked his hair in consolation.

"I am sorry that your teacher treats you in such a disrespectful manner. As an adult, he should set a better example for his students. But how did you get hurt? Surely that didn't come from your teacher."

Pavle shook his head. "No, that comes afterward. Two big boys in the class like to push others around and pick on those who are smaller than them. Ever since the teacher started humiliating me, they have been targeting me. At recess, they taunt me by calling me 'Sabbatarian.' They say our family belongs to a sect. Sometimes the other children join in. And after school . . ."

Pavle trailed off into silence. Anka refilled his cup of tea and waited until he had sipped some of the calming, soothing brew. When his courage was somewhat restored, he continued.

"The two bullies attack me after school. I try to run away as fast as I can, but they are faster. They wait until I am on the long road by the river, where there aren't many houses or people around, and then they beat me up. I don't want to fight them, Mother, but I have to try to defend myself. And that just makes them angrier, and they hit me even harder."

Anka enveloped the boy in a big hug. "There, there," she said. "It's all right. You have done nothing wrong. It was brave of you to stand up to your teacher and the bullies for the Sabbath. This is all their fault. Don't worry. I will talk to your father, and we will figure out a way to protect you from the bullies."

The next day, Milan asked his boss to leave work early to deal with a family emergency. He made his way to the long avenue by the river and hid behind the row of poplars that stood in a column along the bank. He waited patiently in the gathering gloom of the winter afternoon. A farmer passed by on his clattering cart, and a little later, several townspeople headed for their homes. Nobody noticed Milan crouching behind the screen of trees.

Not long afterward, he heard the panicked steps of a desperate flight. It was Pavle, running as fast as his little legs would carry him. Milan waited until his son passed, and then Milan stepped out suddenly into the road in front of the two pursuers, catching them by surprise.

"Good evening, boys," he said pleasantly. "Where are you going in such a hurry? Are you trying to catch up with Pavle to keep him safe on his way back home? Such big, strong boys like you are very eager to guard those who are smaller and weaker, right?"

The bullies said nothing, staring up at the larger figure looming over them in the growing darkness. Milan abruptly changed his tone.

"Shame on you," he said, "beating up a child smaller than yourselves! Why don't you try beating me up? After all, I am also a 'Sabbatarian,' and I do not work on Saturday, just like Pavle. Well, come on!"

The boys exchanged sullen looks.

"What's wrong?" asked Milan. "I hear you usually have a lot of things to say to Sabbath keepers during recess. Where is your courage now?"

One of the boys mumbled something.

"What's that? What did you say?"

"I'm sorry," he said and elbowed the other, who echoed him.

"Good," said Milan as he crossed his brawny arms and glared down at them. "Stay that way. And if I ever hear about this happening again,

I will go and talk to both of your parents, who I know are good people who raised you better than this. Now go and try not to abuse those who are different from you."

Turning, the two boys fled into the twilight as quickly as they had come. Down the road, Milan found Pavle waiting for him.

"Thank you, Father," Pavle said.

"You're welcome," Milan responded, taking his son's hand. "I don't think you have to worry about those two anymore. My scolding seems to have put them in their place."

"What about my teacher?"

"That you will have to endure. There are men at my workplace who do the same to me. They hurt me with words. All we can do is bear it and try to forgive them. This is what God, who forgives us our sins, asks of us. Maybe with time and through your long-suffering witness, your teacher will see that he is wronging you and repent. Do you think you can do this?"

"Yes, Father," Pavle answered, filled with a newfound strength after that afternoon's triumph. Hand in hand, they walked through the dusk toward home.

* * * * *

Just as Milan endured persecution in the workplace, his children endured it in school and sometimes in their neighborhood. Milan and Anka's decision to follow God impacted the entire family. At first, life was very difficult. Pavle's experience was just one of many that tested the faith of the little ones and their parents.

Unfortunately, many people chose to take out their personal problems on the small, isolated group of believers. The new community of faith was an easy target for those entrenched in tradition. Anyone who needed an outlet could funnel their rage at the seemingly unprotected band. And some of the harshest persecution came from within their family circle—an even greater test for Milan and his young family.

Vida's conversion

Milan hesitated before the front door of his mother's house. He came bearing gifts from Anka: a freshly baked loaf of bread, crispy vegetable patties, and cakes. Anka insisted that they keep on good terms with Vida, and though Milan wished with all his heart to comply, it was difficult. Every time he met his mother, she had something negative to say about his newfound faith and lifestyle. Shaking his head free of misgivings, Milan knocked and then entered his old home.

As usual, the house was full of cigarette smoke. Unwashed dishes were piled high in the kitchen sink. The rug by the door was full of dirt and caked with mud. In one corner sat Vida. She lived alone since her daughters had left to start their own families. Beside her on the table was an opened, half-empty bottle.

"Good evening, Mother," Milan greeted her.

Vida grunted a greeting.

"I brought you some bread and cakes. Anka made them. She and the children send you their greetings."

Another grunt. Vida lit a cigarette, inhaled, and immediately started coughing. Her coughs were deep and raspy, convulsing her entire frame with spasms. When the coughing stopped, she spit into a rag. Even in the dim light, Milan could see that the rag was darkly stained.

Milan took his seat in a chair by the window, as close to fresh air as possible. Vida continued to smoke, but her fingers trembled with the effort to suppress her coughs.

"Mother, what are you doing to yourself? Can't you see that your lifestyle is destroying you?"

"It is my life," Vida snapped. "This is how I have always lived. Who are you to tell me otherwise?"

"Don't you remember," Milan spoke gently, "how I used to struggle with smoking and the memories of the war? For a while, I was in a really bad place. But then, in the midst of my despair, God found me and changed my life. If He can save me, He can save you, too."

"Hmph!" Vida snorted. "Keep your strange, foreign beliefs to yourself. What would the neighbors think if I adopted the ways of that sect you are in?"

"Please, Mother. Don't be mean. I am just trying to help."

"Well, you aren't. You come here bringing gifts, but really what you want to do is convert me. You want to turn me into a laughingstock. How could I ever show my face in town again if I were known to be a sectarian?" Vida choked on her words as another extended coughing fit tore through her. Again, she spit into the rag when she was done.

"You are sick," Milan replied. "All this smoking and drinking is killing you. Why don't you give God a chance? He is the Great Healer. He will heal your heart, and maybe your body, too."

"I don't need your God. I don't need your unorthodox religion. I have told you before, but you never listen. Go! Leave me in peace. If that is all you have to say to me, don't bother coming here again."

Sadly, Milan got up to leave. In the doorway, he turned and made a final plea.

"If you won't listen to me, at least go to the hospital. Maybe you will listen to them."

He left her, his steps heavy with the resistance to God encountered in his own family.

A few days later, Vida sat in a hospital bed. The bottle was gone, and so were the cigarettes. But the cough remained—though now she spit into a little basin instead of a rag. A nurse came into the room.

"You have a couple of visitors, Vida," she said. "They say your son sent them. Can they come in?"

Vida nodded, and a couple of gray-haired, neatly attired men walked in. They smiled at Vida, but she retained her sour look.

"What do you want with me? Did Milan send you to say, 'I told you so'?"

"Dear Mother," said one of the men softly, "we have come to comfort you and offer you hope. Milan is very worried about you, but he is afraid that his presence would upset you. So he asked us if we would come and pray with you."

Vida was silent as she stared out the window for a while. The elders waited patiently, respectfully.

"I don't know why you bothered," she finally responded. "I am finished. The doctor says I have at best some weeks left to live. It is too late."

She clutched the bedsheets in desperation as another coughing fit seized her. The elders came closer.

"It is never too late for God. He is the Great Physician. The Bible is full of stories of His healing power. All you have to do is accept His grace. Will you let us pray for you?"

Vida slowly loosened her grip on the bedsheets.

"Why not," she muttered sullenly. "What other choice do I have?"

Smiling gently, the elders took her trembling hands and prayed, "Dear heavenly Father, You know the sufferings of this child of Yours. Please heal her and restore her to health if it is Your will. Her family misses her and loves her very much. And we know that You love her very much as well. Change her heart and grant her new hope, we pray. In Jesus' name, amen."

To her own surprise, Vida echoed, "Amen."

A few days later, Milan received a call to the hospital. When he got there, he found Vida waiting for him at the main entrance. She flew down the stairs and gave him a great big hug. Milan was stunned.

"Mother, what's going on? Shouldn't you be in bed?"

Vida laughed. "No, praise God; I feel so much better."

"What?"

"The doctor says I am on the road to recovery." Vida beamed at Milan, her usually sour face transformed by an inner radiance.

"I don't understand," said Milan slowly. "Didn't you have a serious lung disease?"

"Yes, I did. But not anymore. After those two wonderful elders came and prayed with me, I felt better. That night I slept more soundly than I have in many years. And this morning, I felt so good that I insisted on having a full checkup. That's when the doctor discovered how much my situation has improved."

"How is that possible?" marveled Milan.

Vida laughed again. "With God, anything is possible. Come on, let's go."

"Where to? Your house is in the opposite direction."

"To your church, of course," said Vida. "The first thing I am going to do is thank God and tell Him that I will be baptized into His family. Come on!"

* * * * *

The doctor estimated that Vida had several weeks to live. Instead, she went on to live another fifteen years—and those years were the best of her life. She completely changed. Her negative, antisocial attitude was gone, replaced by kindness and generosity. She joined the church and became a pillar of faith and a living testament to the power of God to heal and transform lives. Instead of drinking and smoking daily, she praised and prayed with fervent regularity. God's Word became central to her everyday life.

To help Milan's ever-growing family, Vida had her old house demolished and gave them the land. When the new family house was built, one room was set aside for her. For the remaining fifteen years of her life, she was an integral part of the family, helping to care for and support the children and guiding them in the pathways of faith. And when two of her grandchildren decided to become ministers, she regularly sent them an allowance out of her pension.

In the neighborhood and throughout the rest of the town, the word spread about Vida's miraculous transformation. Slowly but surely, her reputation changed. If her old, bitter, broken character was ever recalled, it was only to highlight the virtues of her new life.

Sometimes her old customers would seek her out for fortune-telling. On those occasions, Vida took the opportunity to witness to them.

Instead of filling their desperate hearts with lies and tricks, she shared the truth of God's love and the hope of a better life in Jesus Christ. For the little group of believers in Derventa, there was no better proof of the value of their beliefs and lifestyle than the wondrous turnaround of Vida by the healing power of the Great Physician.

CHAPTER SEVEN

THE CHURCH GROWS

The righteous person may have many troubles,
but the LORD delivers him from them all.

—Psalm 34:19

The dedication

On a bright spring afternoon, Milan stood in the Muslim cemetery that lay across the street from his home. Lately, he had been going there to speak with one of his neighbors, who grazed his cows in the meadow surrounding the graves. The man wore a fez wrapped in broad white cloth. This, and the title he went by, Hajji—meaning one who has made the Muslim pilgrimage to Mecca—signified his honorific rank in the Islamic community of the town.

While the cows munched, moving patiently about with swishing tails, Milan and the Hajji discussed many religious matters. For Milan, this was a rare chance to speak with a person of religious authority since the Orthodox and Catholic priests treated him like a heretic. For the Hajji, this was a rare chance to speak with a devout Christian since the Muslims were looked on as little better than heathens. The two men tended to talk about matters of faith on which they agreed: dietary standards, abstaining from harmful substances, and the prophets found in both the Bible and the Quran. Sometimes, however, they stumbled across areas on which they differed. More than once, the Hajji asked with a twinkle in his eye, "How can God have a Son if He has no wife?"

Milan answered, "Are we not all His children? Who, then, is our mother?" And they amicably agreed to disagree.

Meanwhile, the little Adventist community of faith was growing in Derventa. Thanks to the transformative power of the Holy Spirit, who changed the lives of the first believers in positive ways that couldn't be ignored by the community, new members joined the fold. And as their numbers grew, so did their reputation for living clean, honest, and upright lives. Eventually, the happy day came when the town officials decided to grant the church official religious status and allow them to have a public place of worship. Up to that point, they had always met informally in the homes of various families of the faithful. Now they gathered to dedicate, exclusively to the worship of God, the living room of the most prosperous church member, who had a large house on the town's main thoroughfare.

It was a joyous occasion. The local district pastor from the city of Banja Luka came and brought with him a youth choir. The place of worship was crammed from the podium to the back row with believers from the town and the surrounding countryside—young and old, rich and poor, in ones and twos and entire families. All joined in worship to thank God for His blessing in swelling their numbers and granting them a safe place to meet in fellowship. Everyone was thrilled to gather in a place with actual pews and a real pulpit. No longer did they have to moderate their voices. Now their praises soared to the heavens in gratitude to God. For Milan and Anka and their children, this was a day they would never forget. Many in attendance were moved to tears.

As a courtesy, the believers invited the religious authorities of all three major faiths in town. But only one community leader chose to come. He appeared during the song service, his figure made conspicuous by the white cloth wrapped around his fez. It was the Hajji. First, he went to Milan's side and gripped him by the arm as he whispered words of congratulations and encouragement. Then, invited to the platform to give a dedicatory blessing, he took the pulpit. As he raised his hands, the congregation bowed their heads.

"Great God, we are gathered here today to consecrate this place of worship. Bless it and fill it with Your presence so that those who worship here may be blessed as well. Almighty Lord, many are Your children; thank You for loving all of us, different though we may be. As we unite in our love for You, our Father, may we learn to love each other, our brothers and sisters."

"Amen," the congregation responded in unison.

* * * * *

The dedication of the first official registered place of worship was a key moment in the development of the little church. It represented the legitimization and acceptance of their faith in society and displayed the boundless power of God. He had brought His children from the humblest of beginnings—being baptized in isolation and the secrecy of night—to having a place of worship in the center of town.

Furthermore, the inclusion of the Hajji, a person of authority and prestige from another faith, showed the Holy Spirit's power in working through the witnessing of a humble servant such as Milan. The church was growing, in members and in friends.

Finding a fellow believer

Milan raced along the sidewalk, dodging other pedestrians and threading through the many stalls clustered around the bus station. He must not be late! Milan had planned everything perfectly to be able to get home, eat, wash, change, and make it to church just in time. But he needed to hurry.

"Sir, sir! Wait a moment, please," a man, a farmer by his overalls and the hoe and spade in his hands, shouted at Milan. Though it pained him to do so, Milan stopped and turned to the man.

"Can . . . I . . . help you?" Milan managed between panting breaths.

"Yes, please," said the man. "Forgive me for bothering you. I can see you are in a rush. But I need help, and you seem like a person who would be willing to help."

"Certainly," Milan replied, though he wished to get back home as fast as possible. "How can I help you?"

"Well, you see, I came here from my village to do some work. But it took longer than I anticipated, and I missed the last bus home. I don't know anyone here, and I don't know where to spend the night until the next bus tomorrow morning. Would you be so kind as to help me out? I know this is asking a lot."

"It is nothing," said Milan. "God will ask me someday what I have done for His children in need. The least I can do is offer you shelter and food for the night."

"Thank you," said the man. "You are very kind."

"You're welcome. My name is Milan."

"I am Fabian."

The two shook hands, and Milan explained why he was in a rush. He told Fabian about the special meeting that evening at the church, a meeting that was part of a larger evangelistic series.

"If you come to my church on the main street, I will be there in less than an hour. After the meeting, there will be a meal and fellowship, and I am sure that we will be able to find a safe place for you to spend the night."

Fabian thanked Milan, and they parted for the time being.

About an hour later, a breathless but fed, washed, and freshly dressed Milan arrived at the church. It was full of people. Extra chairs had been brought to accommodate everyone, and the overflow was such that people were standing on the porch, peering through the opened windows. Milan squeezed through the crowd and spotted Fabian sitting near the front. Somehow, he had managed to save Milan a chair. Together, they sat and listened to the pastor's presentation on God's unfailing love for us and our grateful response to Him.

After the presentation, most of the congregation left, but Milan and Fabian stayed for the after-meeting with the pastor and several attendees interested in learning more. Fabian listened politely to the discussion, and when the talk died down, he spoke.

"I have learned a lot today and think that what you are doing is great. However, I am not a religious man. I do not mean any disrespect, but your ways are not for me. I do know of someone, though, whose ways are just like yours. In fact, I am pretty sure he is one of you."

"What?" asked the listeners. "Who is this? How can there be another believer we do not know about?"

"Let me tell you," said Fabian. A meal was served for those who had stayed on, and he spoke while he wolfed down his food. "This is wonderful, wonderful!" he exclaimed. The others laughed and restrained their curiosity at his strange words. With a full mouth and a rapidly filling belly, Fabian told them.

"His name is Ivan. He is well known in my village as a good man and a hard worker. He is very honest and will never cheat anyone.

"Some years ago, he lost his wife to disease. This was a very difficult time for him. During his depression, he turned to God and prayed for deliverance. God spoke to him in a dream and told him to get a Bible. So, Ivan went to the priest. At first, the priest hesitated to give him a Bible. This is not customary for those of the traditional faith. But when Ivan told him of his dream, the priest relented and gave Ivan a Bible.

"Ivan was never the same. He began to read his Bible carefully, and soon his whole lifestyle changed. Ivan doesn't work on Saturday. He doesn't eat unhealthy foods or drink alcohol. Ivan prays only to God and His Son, Jesus. And he is waiting for Christ's soon return. I tell you, my friends, Ivan is exactly like you!"

Marveling at the miracle, Milan and a couple of the elders decided to take Fabian back to his village the next day to see for themselves. After a good night's sleep and a hearty breakfast in a church member's house, Fabian sat in the front passenger seat of an elder's car and was driven back to his village. After dropping him off at his farm, the others followed his directions to the humble abode where Ivan and his family lived.

Jumping out of the car, Milan ran excitedly over to the house and knocked on the front door. Ivan, an older man with a kind smile on his honest face, opened the door and greeted him. When Milan explained what they had heard about him and why they had come all the way from town, Ivan invited them in for tea.

"If what you have said is true, and you really worship God on the seventh-day Sabbath, then we are the same. Come in, my brothers."

Over tea and biscuits, they talked about God's truth and the promises in the Bible. Ivan brought out a worn book and showed them where he had found the instructions from God on how to live a clean and upright life. Milan and his fellow believers were shocked to find that Ivan had discovered and faithfully observed all of God's commandments. But the greatest surprise came at the end.

"Now," said Ivan, "let me show you something."

They followed him to the pantry, where he indicated a shelf loaded with farm produce and preserves. At the end of the shelf was a heap of money.

"This is my tithe for the past three years," Ivan informed them. "Ever since I read about it in the Word of God, I have been keeping it in anticipation of the day when I would meet other children of the Lord. And now the blessed day has come. Please, accept this humble gift of mine and take my tithes and offerings for the church."

With praise spilling from their mouths and joy filling their hearts, the believers accepted Ivan's tithe and welcomed him into God's family.

* * * * *

Though there were numerous conversion experiences during the early years of the church's growth in Derventa, Ivan's story stood out. No other story displayed the power of God as Ivan's did. For, thanks to the wonderful work of the Holy Spirit, Ivan was ready to join the church when he met the believers. In fact, he had been ready for years before that. Through the message of God in a dream, and the guidance of the Holy Spirit as Ivan studied the Word, his life was completely changed. All that remained was for him to meet and join the growing church family.

Not long after Milan and the elders visited, Ivan and his whole family were baptized into the church. They would prove to be some of the most faithful and fervent believers in the flock. And this unification was possible only because Milan took the time to listen and aid a farmer in need of help by the bus station. Praise the Lord!

A change of plans

It was late in the evening. After Anka put the children to bed, she studied the lesson quarterly with Milan. They were both worn out from the day's labors—Anka's ceaseless work at home and Milan's grueling tasks in the factory. But before they went to bed, they always took time to study God's Word. A knock on the door disturbed their studies. Milan opened the door to find Pavle, now grown into a fine young man, standing in the night, suitcase in hand.

"Pavle! What is going on? Shouldn't you be at school?" asked Milan in wonder.

"Let the child in," said Anka. "Can't you see he is tired from his long journey? Let me get some food into him, and then he can tell us what has happened."

After Pavle had stuffed himself with leftovers from dinner, he sat down on the sofa between his parents and sadly related his story. He was an adult now, much changed from when he was persecuted at school for keeping the Sabbath.

"Everything was going well at first," he said. "I got along with my classmates, and my teachers were impressed with my schoolwork. In fact, I was getting straight As. But then the trouble started. I tried to get ahead of it by talking to the headmaster about my faith and how God wants us to keep the Sabbath. But he wouldn't listen or consider my offers to make up classes on Sundays. When I missed the first Saturday classes, I was warned. When I missed the second, I was formally reprimanded. And when I missed the third, I was summoned before the disciplinary board. They were pretty rough. They told me that my beliefs were getting in the way of my studies and that if I wanted to succeed, I would have to choose between them. They said I had two options: to go to school on the Sabbath or be dismissed from school. I did not hesitate. I chose the latter. I hope I have done well."

"Certainly," said Milan, clapping him on the shoulder. "You have done like the prophets of old, standing up to the rulers of this world for the sake of God's commandments."

"But Father," Pavle said with tears in his eyes, "they said such mean things after I made my decision. They told me I would never amount to anything, that my faith was a joke, and that I would end up a failure. And when I left the school grounds, some jeered and mocked."

Anka gave the young man a hug, and Milan squeezed his hand.

"Never mind," said Anka. "You cannot control what others do or say. All you can control are your own actions. And you have done what is right. God will reward you; you'll see."

"But what will I do now?" Pavle wondered. "How can I ever get a decent job if I can't finish school?"

"My son," Milan said quietly but firmly, "I cannot make that decision for you. But what I can tell you is this: whatever you decide to be in life, if God is on your side, no one will be able to stop you.

"Listen! There was a time, when you were still in elementary school, that our church faced heavy persecution. Do you remember when you were bullied at school, and I had to put those bullies in their place? Well, that was what happened on the ground level. But there were other problems, further up, that threatened our freedom and our faith from the highest levels of authority. One Sabbath, the conference president's assistants came to church and informed us to be prepared for serious persecution. They said that a law was about to be passed to allow the imprisonment of parents whose children routinely missed school. On the surface, this law was meant to protect children whose parents deprived them of education to make them work on the farms during harvest. But in reality, this law could pave the way to the persecution of the church, which was growing rapidly in the region, something not appreciated by the atheistic government and the traditional religions."

Anka shook her head in remembrance of those trying times.

"What were we to do?" continued Milan. "Most of us were terrified at the idea of going to jail. Then a couple of us got together, prayed to the Lord for guidance and strength, and resolved to rise to the occasion. All of us who had been in the war, the veterans from the churches in the area, got together and went to the Ministry of the Interior in Sarajevo. There we appealed to the highest judges in the region, shared with them our faith and reasons for keeping the Sabbath, and explained how precarious our position was. And guess what? God heard our cry for help and intervened on our behalf. The judges relented and overturned the law. We went from fearing for our safety to changing the laws of the land, just because we put our trust in God."

"That is incredible," Pavle said, his eyes shining with hope. "If God could help you with such a huge problem, how could He not aid me with my little one?"

Bowing their heads together, Milan, Anka, and Pavle prayed to the Lord for help. Then they went to bed, safe in the assurance that whatever happened would be according to His will.

The next morning, the whole family was gathered at the dining table when Pavle made his announcement.

"As you all know, yesterday I came home because I was dismissed from school for keeping the Sabbath. At first, I was disappointed, thinking that the only path left for me in life was to become a day laborer and struggle for my existence. But then father told me a wonderful story of how he and other church members had been part of a miracle that God had worked for our deliverance when we were facing harsh persecution. So, as I lay in bed last night, I decided to dedicate my life to the Lord and become a minister. I do not know how I will be able to pay for my studies, but I will work hard and leave the rest in God's hands."

"Amen!" Milan and the rest of the family said together, inspired by Pavle's bold plan and faith in God's guidance.

* * * * *

Just as God helped the church members when they were facing imprisonment for keeping the Sabbath, so He helped Pavle when he decided to dedicate his life to the ministry in response to being dismissed from school for keeping the Sabbath. The God who delivered before would deliver again.

Not long after Pavle made his decision, the conference selected him to be one of the three youths from the entire region to be sent to study at the theological seminary in the capital city of Belgrade. His studies would be partially sponsored, and to cover the rest of his expenses, a local church member hired Pavle to help build chimneys all summer before classes started in the fall. With the help of God and the church, and with a lot of hard work and determination on his part, Pavle was able to take the first step toward the realization of his dream: to serve God as one of His ministers. Thereby was the dismissal from school for keeping the Sabbath turned into an unfathomable blessing.

Witnessing at work

Milan wiped the sweat off his face. It was hot and humid in the factory, and he was working hard, welding and moving large pieces of machinery. A shrill whistle signaled a short break. All around him, men sat down to rest—but not Milan. He headed straight to his locker, pulled out a bundle of pamphlets, and started circulating among his coworkers.

"Hello, Bogdan, nice to see you. I hope you are doing well. Do you know that God cares for you and has a special plan for you? Here, please take this and read it. It will show you God's love."

"Good morning, Miroslav. I trust all is well with you and your family. Do you know that you belong to a greater family and that God is your Father? Here, this tract will tell you more. I would be very happy if you took a look at it."

"Tihomir, my friend. You look much better than the last time I saw you. Do you know that God has made special rules to keep us healthy and happy? Please accept this little book. It will show you how to live life fully."

Most of the men were unresponsive; they took the pamphlets but didn't show any interest. A few turned their backs as soon as Milan approached and ignored him. One openly laughed in Milan's face and tossed the tract in a nearby trash can. Milan silently retrieved it, dusted it off, and continued with his witnessing. He did this every day during every break, but sometimes he wondered what the point was. It seemed that the more he tried to reach out to his coworkers, the less responsive they became. It was almost as if his efforts had hardened their hearts against God instead of drawing them to Him.

The whistle shrieked again, signaling that the break was over. Milan rushed back to his workstation, gulping down some water on the way. Sometimes he forgot to hydrate, so fervent was his zeal to share the gospel during the breaks.

He reached for his visor and torch, but they shifted from under his hand. The floor beneath his feet shivered. Loud clangs echoed through the factory's halls, and the shouts and screams of men were lost in the cacophonous din. Realizing that an earthquake was happening, Milan dropped to his knees and prayed for deliverance.

A moment later, it was all over. The damage was minimal: a few broken tools, some disconnected machinery, several bruised workers. While the supervisors got everyone back to work, Milan thanked God for His protection and then focused on his welding. Hours later, another break was called. As usual, Milan went to his locker for his witnessing materials. But before he made it, he was surrounded by his coworkers.

"Comrade Milan, we saw you on your knees during the earthquake. While we were all running to save ourselves, you were praying to your God. Tell us more about this wondrous faith of yours."

"Milan, you are always warning us of the disasters that will happen before the return of Christ. Is this one of them?"

"I am frightened, Milan. I thought I was going to die and never get to fix all the wrong things I have done in my life. Tell me, how can I make things right before it is too late?"

The shaken men pressed him with questions, suddenly eager to learn from the person they had either merely tolerated or outright shunned for so long. With a humble smile, Milan politely asked them to let him through to his locker. Then he handed out the pamphlets until none were left and began sharing with the avid listeners the story of God's plan of salvation and the good news of Christ's soon return.

* * * * *

Thanks to the earthquake, which shook not only the earth but also the hearts of Milan's coworkers, the Lord was able to reach those who were determined to be unreachable. Sadly, many of the men, when they recovered from their shock and fright, returned to their former heedless state. But others were profoundly moved and kept their hearts open to God's Word.

Eventually, through the work of the Holy Spirit, Milan arranged for Bible studies with two of his coworkers. After some months of deepening friendship and in-depth studies of Scripture, both coworkers and their entire families joined the growing church. That is how God works in this world: through the diligent witnessing of His servants and the miraculous signs of nature.

A community of care

In the bright freshness of a summer morning, several cars pulled up to a little farm some distance from Derventa. Out of the cars spilled numerous children, shouting and laughing in their excitement. They were followed by their parents and other adults, who led them to the humble cottage of Anton and his two sisters. Because the cottage was too small to admit the group, they stood in a circle outside and prayed together after a short devotional by one of the elders. Then they got to work.

Everyone did something. The men went to the fields to dig up potatoes and then stored them in neat rows of sacks. Next, they moved on to harvest the golden corn. Afterward, they husked it and ground it by hand. Then they went to the orchard and collected the ripe plums and picked the juicy apples off the trees. The women milked the cows and baked the corn bread. The children, who had been stuffing themselves on the fruit, were told to mind the cows and goats and lead them to a nearby pasture. There, the kids ran around and played to their hearts' content, rolling around in the grass and chasing butterflies while keeping an eye on the animals.

When the work was done, it was noon and time for fun. The group got together again for a meal of corn bread hot out of the oven and homemade cheese and preserves. When everyone had enough, the games began. There was a short soccer match and an extended swimming session in the broad Sava River that flowed by the farm's pasture. The young adults competed in swimming contests while the children splashed around in the shallows. Finally, when they had tired themselves out, the women brought out tea and cakes to close the gathering with a light meal. Another short devotional was offered by one of the mothers, and after a prayer and a song, the families crowded back into the cars and drove off as the three hosts waved goodbye. Anton and his sisters returned to their cottage, grateful for the community of care that had done a week's worth of farmwork in a single day.

* * * * *

This story illustrates the importance of community in the life of the church in Derventa. Though witnessing and conversion were obviously a fundamental step in the growth of the new group of believers, they would have amounted to little if not sustained by church members caring for one another and helping those who were less fortunate.

Anton and his sisters were converts who were welcomed into the fold with open arms. The three of them had grown up as orphans, losing their father in the war and later their mother to sickness. They had spent most of their lives alone on their farm, occasionally looked after by neighboring relatives and friends but essentially isolated from the rest of society. Anton, the oldest, sought to fill the void in his heart by having as much fun as possible with his friends. When he reached adulthood, he often went into town with a couple of buddies to have a good time. One evening, while they roamed around, they happened to see a poster advertising a church meeting. Just as a joke, they decided to attend. It was a meeting on God's care for us and was held by Pastor Radovan. After half an hour or so, Anton's friends grew bored and left. Anton stayed for the rest of the meeting and for the rest of his life. Eventually, he and his sisters were baptized into the church.

Life on the farm was hard. There was a lot of work to be done, and it had to be done in time for the harvest. So, the church would regularly have outings to Anton's place to help the three siblings and spend time together in a community of care. These gatherings, which were focused on supporting and uplifting the less fortunate, unified the growing church community. Not only did Anton and his sisters become faithful, lifelong members of the church, but those who came to help them, particularly the children, were deeply and positively influenced by those times of Christian fellowship and charitable work. By living Christ's message of hope, the group of believers strengthened one another's faith and showed the world the practical worth of their belief.

CHAPTER EIGHT

A WITNESS IN A TIME OF WAR

Lord, our Lord,
how majestic is your name in all the earth!

You have set your glory
in the heavens.
Through the praise of children and infants
you have established a stronghold against your enemies,
to silence the foe and the avenger.
When I consider your heavens,
the work of your fingers,
the moon and the stars,
which you have set in place,
what is mankind that you are mindful of them,
human beings that you care for them?

You have made them a little lower than the angels
and crowned them with glory and honor.
You made them rulers over the works of your hands;
you put everything under their feet:
all flocks and herds,
and the animals of the wild,
the birds in the sky,
and the fish in the sea,
all that swim the paths of the seas.

Lord, our Lord,
how majestic is your name in all the earth!

—Psalm 8

Whose side are you on?

Milan was in a hurry, pedaling on his bicycle to make it back to his and Anka's apartment before the sun went down. He tried his best to go fast, but he was no longer a young man. In fact, he was rather old now. The children had all grown up and moved away, and Milan and Anka had relocated across the Sava River to the town of Brod in Croatia. This had turned out to be providential, for another war began to plague the region, this time a civil one, and the town of Derventa and the surrounding region of Bosnia had turned into a bloody war zone. But Brod was relatively safe in Croatia, though at times it was bombarded from the other side of the river, and the threat of a possible invasion loomed.

Right at sunset, Milan reached the apartment building. A man was standing by the entrance to the stairway. He was smartly dressed in a formal suit, and though he exuded authority, he had no insignia or badge to mark him as an official. As soon as he saw Milan, he approached.

"Are you the Milan who lives in this building?"

"Yes, I am."

"You have applied for Croatian citizenship. I need to ask you some questions. Is that all right?"

"Certainly," Milan said, locking his bicycle and gesturing toward the stairs. "Please come with me to my place."

In their cozy little apartment, Anka welcomed the official and brought chamomile tea and poppy seed cakes. The man helped himself to both and then, noticing through the window that the sun was setting, sighed and said, "It has been a long day."

"Indeed, it has," Milan agreed. "And I must ask of you a favor before we get to your questions. Tomorrow is Saturday, and my wife and I keep it as the Sabbath, God's holy day of rest. It begins now, at sundown on Friday. Would it be OK with you if we had a short worship service?"

"Sure," the man said. "I've been working all day. I could use a little break."

Milan picked up the Bible that always lay prominently in the middle of the coffee table. Its cover was worn with use, the pages full of underlining and notations.

"This is Psalm Ninty-One," he said. "It is my favorite psalm because it speaks of the care and protection offered by God to us, His children.

> " 'Whoever dwells in the shelter of the Most High
> will rest in the shadow of the Almighty.
> I will say of the LORD, 'He is my refuge and my fortress,
> my God, in whom I trust' " (Psalm 91:1, 2).

When Milan finished, Anka joined him in singing a hymn of praise. Then they bowed their heads to pray. The official bowed his head as well.

"Thank you for letting us worship," Milan said after the prayer was done.

The man waved his hand. "Please, don't mention it. After all those years of state-imposed atheism, it is a pleasure to meet someone who is sincerely religious. In our new country, we value those who believe in God."

He pulled a form out of his briefcase and continued, "Now, Milan, I would like to ask you those questions, though I must say your behavior, along with your wife's, has already put most of my concerns to rest. You see, my department is worried that because you were active during the Second World War and declared yourself as a Yugoslav in the previous census, you might not be qualified for Croatian citizenship. Though it states in our records that you never were a Party member, as you know, Croatia is now at war with that federal army you were once a part of. And you are applying for citizenship. Can you explain these apparent contradictions? Why should we grant you Croatian citizenship? Whose side are you on?"

Milan was silent for a moment. Then he reached for the Bible.

"May I read another passage to you as an explanation of my position on these matters?"

The official nodded assent.

"The apostle John writes: 'Whoever claims to love God yet hates a brother or sister is a liar. For whoever does not love their brother and sister, whom they have seen, cannot love God, whom they have not seen. And he has given us this command: Anyone who loves God must also love their brother and sister' (1 John 4:20, 21). That is my answer. Because I love God, I also love all my fellow human beings, whether they are citizens of the old country or are religious patriots now, whether they reside on the other side or on this side of the river."

The man blinked a couple of times, betraying his surprise at this unconventional and unexpected answer. Then he put his unmarked form back into his briefcase and stood.

"Thank you for your answer and for your hospitality."

"You are welcome," said Milan, escorting him out. "I wish you a happy Sabbath."

Two weeks later, Milan's documents arrived in the mail. By the grace of God, his citizenship application had been successful.

* * * * *

Getting Croatian citizenship during the civil war was not an easy feat. The conflict had turned ugly by that point. In Bosnia, the federal troops were fighting all those who wished to separate themselves from the state. In response, anyone in Croatia with ties to the old regime was looked upon with suspicion. A purge was carried out, and there were horror stories of thugs throwing elderly people off their balconies. People disappeared overnight and were never seen again.

The official's showing up to question Milan meant that the new government had serious questions about his status. Because of his involvement in the previous war, he was likely perceived as a potential traitor and threat to the fledgling nation. But thanks to Milan's sincere witness, the official was wholly won over. It was clear to him that Milan was a man of God and a trustworthy citizen. By mirroring God's love through his life and appealing to the truth of the Bible, Milan was able to prove to the authorities that he was a valuable member of society and deserving of citizenship. Once again, Milan's faith in God had protected him in a time of trouble.

Dushan's story

It was late at night. Milan and Anka were already in bed, sound asleep, when a soft but persistent knocking on the door roused them. Milan answered it to find their son Dushan, the only family member who had stayed in Bosnia after the war started. Underneath a military coat draped over his shoulders, his clothes were torn and filthy as if he had been living outside. His whole body shook uncontrollably, and his face was as white as a sheet.

Milan and Anka took him in and did their best to comfort him. For a week, all he did was sit in the spare bedroom and stare at the wall. He slept little, ate less, and said nothing. Milan and Anka barely recognized their son, the athlete of the family, who once was the star goalie of Derventa's soccer team but now seemed to be a shrunken, diminished person. Not knowing what to do, his parents sang hymns of encouragement and read aloud uplifting passages in the Bible. Finally, after a particularly profound worship service, Dushan opened his mouth and spoke. The words spilled out in a torrent as if he were overcompensating for the long silence. All Milan and Anka could do was listen to the incredible tale.

"As you know, Mom and Dad, I decided to stay in Bosnia to protect my home and business. I had worked and accomplished so much that I could not bear to abandon it all. I sent my family out, but I stayed. At the time, it seemed impossible to me that our sleepy little town could ever be overcome by hatred and violence. But that was exactly what happened. Not long after I sent my family away to safety, various paramilitary groups arrived and started a bitter fight for control of the town. Many houses were destroyed, and many parts of town became dangerous. I spent a couple of months in the basement with several neighbors of different faiths and cultures. We ventured out only to get food and water, which became harder and harder to find. Every day we lived in fear. I was surrounded by enemies on all sides. Because our family name is Orthodox, the federal troops might grab me, forcefully enlist me, and send me to certain death on the front line. Or the Catholics and Muslims might consider me an enemy and kill me on the spot. The worst was when childhood friends, people who had gone to school with me and lived their whole lives in my neighborhood, turned against me and conspired to have me killed simply because my ethnic or religious background was different from theirs.

"One day, a truck full of paramilitary soldiers loyal to the old regime pulled up. They gathered all the men in my neighborhood and started distributing weapons. I knew that they were going to send us to the front. I did not know what to do. So, I closed my eyes and prayed silently to God for help. When the soldiers came to me, they pressed the rifle into my hands. I refused to take it. They began to curse at me and threaten me, calling me a traitor for not fighting for my ethnic group. But the neighbors put up a protest and told the soldiers that because of my faith, I could not bear arms and fight against those whom I considered to be fellow children of God. My neighbors, God bless them, insisted that I belong to a church of peace and love. The soldiers were not happy, but they settled on making me responsible for delivering supplies to various units in town instead of fighting on the front. God must have been watching over me.

"Eventually, the fighting got so bad that I knew I had to leave while I still had my life. The paramilitary groups were reducing the town to rubble. Those civilians who still remained were informing on one another just to stay alive. The closest way to safety was over the Sava River and into Croatia. But the bridge was controlled by soldiers who would not let me cross the border. I had to try, however. At least there was a chance, though it was small. If I stayed in town, there was no chance. I would certainly be killed as so many of my neighbors and friends had been.

"I took all the money I had and my documents and set off on foot. It took me many days to cover the twenty miles between Derventa and here. There were roadblocks everywhere, fields and forests had been mined, and it seemed that snipers were lurking in every shadowed spot. Sometimes I would sleep in abandoned buildings, but mostly I slept outside, in the rain and mud, always on the run. There wasn't much to eat, but I managed to find enough in abandoned houses to keep me on my feet. When I finally got to the bridge, I was exhausted to the point of collapse, but I knew that if I could just manage to make it across to you, I would be safe for the time being.

"On the bridge, I joined a mass of people trying to get across. It was chaotic. Everyone was desperate to get away from the horrors of the war. But the soldiers stopped us and started dividing us into two groups. Women and children were allowed to get through, but all able-bodied men were turned back. My heart was filled with dread. As soon as the soldiers figured out who I was, they assigned me to the group that was to go back to Bosnia in military trucks that were obviously headed for the front. I began to panic, knowing this was basically a death sentence. The federal troops view us as deserters who deserved to be sent to the most dangerous battle zones.

"Suddenly, a man materialized next to me. He was tall and dressed in the uniform of a military officer. He yelled my name, apparently recognizing me though I had never seen him before in my life. 'Get out of here, Dushan,' he said to me. Then he took off his officer's coat, put it on me, and pushed me toward the checkpoint. As if in a dream, I walked through the border. The same guards that had just sent me back now waved me through, barely glancing at my documents or my face. With my mind reeling and my legs wobbling, I somehow made it across the bridge and to your apartment. I have no idea who that man was or how he saved me from certain death. It is beyond understanding."

"Praise the Lord!" exclaimed Anka, taking Dushan's shaking hands in hers.

"It must have been an angel, sent to protect you like the angels who guarded Daniel in the lions' den," Milan said. "We must thank God for His protection."

Overcome by the trauma of his harrowing experience and the unexpectedness of his deliverance, Dushan put his face in his hands and wept.

For the next week, Dushan stayed with his parents, recovering from his ordeal and gathering strength for the next stage of his journey.

Though he had escaped the terrible situation in Bosnia, he wasn't in the clear yet. Armed bands were constantly making their way through Brod and the surrounding countryside, searching for anyone who did not have Croatian documents. Dushan knew that he must leave soon, not only for his safety but also for the safety of his parents, who were harboring him.

The day came when he had to leave to make his way to the border of Slovenia. Anka tearfully bade him farewell and pressed a bundle of food into his hands. Milan accompanied his son. The plan was to get to Zagreb, the capital, by bus and then take a ride with a Danish church member, Leah, out of Croatia. Getting on the bus was easy. No one bothered to check Dushan's documents, which were from the old regime and clearly showed that he didn't have Croatian heritage. But as the bus headed down the small country lanes toward Zagreb, since the highway had been bombed, it became clear that only a miracle would save Dushan.

Every dozen miles or so, the bus was stopped at a checkpoint, and soldiers boarded to check everyone's documents. At the first of these, Dushan sat frozen in his seat with fear. In desperation, Milan draped his coat over Dushan and tried to conceal him with the suitcase. They were sitting at the back of the bus and the light was dim, but only a blind man could miss the brawny man sitting next to Milan. Both of them prayed, asking God to shelter Dushan in this time of great peril.

The soldiers boarded and made their way to the back of the bus, and Milan handed them his Croatian documents. They glanced at the documents, returned them, and left without saying a word about Dushan. It was almost as if they did not even see the sizable form on the seat next to Milan. Dushan breathed a sigh of relief—God had saved him! This happened again and again, checkpoint after checkpoint, until they reached the Zagreb bus station. Not far from there, near a little park, the car that would transport Dushan across the border waited. Beside the car stood Leah, a church member from Denmark who made the border crossing weekly. If Dushan was to have a chance to get to safety, it would be with her. Milan grasped his son's hand as they parted. Dushan tearfully thanked his father and promised to let him know when he reached safety. Then he was off, and Milan was left to return to Brod alone, with a heart full of worry and anxiety for Dushan's welfare.

The next few days were agonizing for Milan and Anka. Doubt gnawed at them, and terrible fears assailed them. Finally, the phone rang and broke the suspense. It was Dushan! He was safe and sound in Slovenia and had a bright joyfulness in his voice as he recounted the last stage of his trip.

"It was amazing. Only the power of God could have brought me out of Bosnia and through all the checkpoints on our way to Zagreb, and only the power of God could have seen me across the last border to Slovenia. Before we tried to cross, Leah and I prayed. Because she is from Denmark and has a house in Slovenia, she crosses the border frequently and is well known by the guards. Also, her car's license plate is Slovenian. These things were in our favor. But what she was doing was illegal. My documents were no longer recognized by either Croatia or Slovenia since the old regime had collapsed. If they discovered who I was, I would have been sent back to Bosnia, and Leah would have been jailed. Still, God gave her the strength to help me. I owe my life to her and to Him.

"When we got to the border, we could see that the guards were stopping all the cars and doing detailed searches. They were making the passengers get out and searching the vehicles. The car directly in front of us was ripped apart. But God's protecting angels were with us. Leah put her Danish passport on top of mine and handed it to the guard, greeting him by name since she crossed the border so frequently. He took one look at her passport, handed it back to her without checking mine, and then waved us through. That was it! I was free! And now I am safe with my family."

Dushan choked with emotion on the phone. On the other end, Milan and Anka were crying as well. All they could do was rejoice in their son's deliverance and praise God for His protection. Before Dushan hung up, they prayed together in thankfulness to the Lord for delivering Dushan from the depths of the war and bringing him through seemingly impossible obstacles to freedom.

* * * * *

The story of Dushan's escape was one more example in Milan's life of God's care for him and his family. That terrible war pitted neighbors against one another and claimed many innocent lives in Bosnia and the surrounding countries. But thanks to the power of God, Dushan was spared, not once but numerous times. Even though he lost everything he owned—his house, his business, and his savings—Dushan was able to keep his life. And through his miraculous deliverance, he found a strengthened faith in the God who had saved him—a faith that would enable him to start a new life abroad in Austria. Dushan went on to prosper greatly in everything he put his hand to until he doubled what he had lost to the war in Bosnia. And he never forgot that he owed everything he had to God.

Later in life, after the war had stopped and the survivors began to rebuild the war-torn country, Dushan returned many times to his hometown with a pickup and trailer full of medical, school, and personal supplies for the local hospitals. His generosity was a tremendous blessing to the people in his former hometown. Dushan never boasted; instead, he chose to remind his neighbors that it was all possible because the Lord had rescued him and blessed him with the chance to rebuild his life. Through the testimony of his miraculous story of deliverance and his Christian charity afterward, many people saw the true light of the love of Christ.

Unshakable faith

As the bombs fell on Brod, Milan and Anka sat in the damp basement of their apartment building and prayed for God's protection. Their location was bad—they were situated between a military camp and a factory, a prime target for the artillery of the federalist forces on the other side of the river. But still, they were grateful to be alive and have a place to hide. They had heard terrible stories of the bombardment of a stadium where refugees were sheltered. As the months passed and the war dragged on, the fighting got more desperate, and the atrocities became more heinous. What a trial for Milan and Anka to pass through in their old age!

Finally, the bombs stopped falling and the sirens ceased wailing. Milan and Anka waited. After an hour of stillness, they ventured out of the basement with the rest of their neighbors. Anka started up the stairway to inspect their home while Milan grabbed his bicycle and headed out the front door.

"What are you doing?" Anka gasped. "Don't you know they might start bombing again at any moment? Where will you hide if you are caught outside?"

"Brother Slavko is too frail to go out to get basic supplies. And sister Mira lost her children in the war and has no one to bring her food," said Milan. "Do not worry, I am doing the Lord's work and will trust Him to protect His servant."

As Milan pedaled off, swerving to avoid the bomb craters in the street, Anka said a silent prayer for his safety. He made it to the store and was fortunate enough not to have to wait too long until the owner showed up to reopen it. After loading his bike with bread and milk, Milan headed for the homes of those he was trying to help. But he didn't get very far.

As he crossed a major intersection, the air-raid sirens began to howl, and the pedestrians scattered. Before Milan could figure out where to hide, a bomb hit the other side of the road. He was violently thrown off his bicycle. Dazed, he first thought that it was merely the blast that knocked him down. But as the shock faded and his senses returned, an ever-growing pain alerted him to the fact that he had been wounded. Shrapnel from the bomb had cut into his side and blown off the thumb and index finger on his right hand. Weak and dizzy from his fall and loss of blood, all Milan could do was sit there.

A police car pulled up, and two heavily armed officers jumped out. They quickly wrapped his hand and bandaged his side as best they could. Then they put him in the back seat and drove off with flashing lights and screaming sirens toward the hospital. Bombs were still falling as they rattled across the damaged roads of the city. One of the officers looked back at Milan to check on him. Shaking his head, the man marveled at the horrors of war. Then his tone changed from dismay to rage. He began cursing, first the violence, then the enemy, and finally God. He used the strongest language he knew as he cursed God for the atrocities suffered by the innocent during that horrible war.

"Stop the car!" Milan shouted above the cursing and explosions.

"What?" the policeman asked.

"I said stop the car," Milan repeated.

"What for? We must get you to the hospital as soon as possible. Are you still in shock? Don't you know that you are bleeding dangerously?"

"Don't worry about me. I want you to stop the car so that I can get out."

"Have you lost your mind, old man? Do you want to get hit by another bomb or bleed to death on the street?"

"Never mind," said Milan stubbornly. "I would rather take my chances out there alone than stay here in a car in which my God is cursed."

The policeman who cursed God was silent. Then the other one spoke.

"What you are saying is right. I should have said it myself to my friend here. What is happening in this war is not God's fault. This is all done by us, not by God."

"Yes," agreed the first policeman. "Both of you are right. I am sorry for what I have said."

He turned to Milan and took him by his unwounded hand.

"Please forgive me and stay in the car."

"God forgives us all," Milan said to him. "Thank you for listening to me, and thank you for rescuing me. Do you not see how God has used you to save me? Amid all this suffering and death, God is still able to help us when we choose to do His will."

Deep in thought and with all curses banished from their lips, the policemen completed the drive and delivered Milan safely to the hospital.

* * * * *

Throughout his life, Milan's primary purpose was to witness to others and share the love of God with them. He did this not only by sharing religious literature but also by living his life as an example of the power of God. There were those in the church who disagreed with his methods, but Milan believed in the transformative influence of the Holy Spirit. This is why he tried to reach out to people on a personal level and show them that there was a better way of living life, a life in accordance with God's instructions. And so Milan witnessed in every deed and with every word. The story of how he confronted his rescuers after he was wounded by the bomb is perhaps the most dramatic of these. Amid great suffering and fear, Milan gave witness to these two men and turned their hearts toward God. Only by constantly trusting God and daily committing his life to Him was Milan able to accomplish this great act of faith.

CHAPTER NINE

A LIFE OF FAITH

Yet I am always with you;
you hold me by my right hand.
You guide me with your counsel,
and afterward you will take me into glory.
Whom have I in heaven but you?
And earth has nothing I desire besides you.
My flesh and my heart may fail,
but God is the strength of my heart
and my portion forever.

—Psalm 73:23–26

Restoring the church

Milan and Anka's living room was full of church members. Extra chairs were brought in from the kitchen, and the bedrooms were opened so that people could sit on the beds. The meeting was a lively one, even though most of the believers wore dour faces.

"I am glad they have left," declared an older man. "They were more trouble than they were worth."

"Yes," agreed a matron next to him. "And I have a feeling they weren't there out of a sincere desire to learn more about God. They just came for the food and to get off the street."

"Excuse me," one man said, "but as you know, I have just returned to town after a long trip abroad. I do not understand what is going on. Why are we meeting here instead of the church? And what are you talking about? It almost sounds as if the church has been taken over by some other group."

"By rascals!" scoffed a feisty believer. "They turned our church into a nightclub!"

"Please, brothers and sisters, calm yourselves," one of the elders said. "Let me explain to our friend exactly what happened. Maybe this recollection will help us decide how to move on from here."

"There's nothing left to move on to, not after the shame that has been brought on us. The whole neighborhood is talking," muttered someone in a corner. But the others shushed him, and the elder began to speak.

"It all started when we got our new pastor. He is a good man, a man of God, who cares deeply for the downtrodden. Now, he wished to reach those on the bottom rung of society. Accordingly, he came up with a plan to open the doors of our church to the homeless and the addicted. And I mean this literally. Some of us supported this idea because the point of the gospel is to spread the good news to others and not hoard it to ourselves. Converting the church into a shelter for the most oppressed of God's children was appealing to us. But others were not too thrilled about this because they feared the situation could get out of hand and our reputation in town would be tarnished."

Pointed coughs could be heard around the room. The elder ignored them and continued. "At first, things went really well. There was some tension over the music used to attract the people off the streets, but the large numbers that came could not be disputed. Even those who were most opposed could not argue that the new pastor was not reaching unprecedented numbers of people with this new approach. It was quite uplifting to see the church grounds full of people fellowshiping and discussing the Word of God. But then things got out of hand. Despite his best intentions, the pastor really had no experience dealing with large numbers of people with serious behavioral issues. Soon, many of them started showing up drunk or high on drugs. The song service became wilder and wilder. The bathroom facilities were trashed, as were the church's grounds, and none of our guests ever offered to clean up after themselves. Worst of all, our reputation began to seriously deteriorate! For decades, our believers have carefully cultivated a reputation of clean, honest, and respectable living. Though not belonging to any of the traditional religions, our church was known to be a place of sober and serious worship. Now it had become a dirty and riotous place. People began crossing to the other side of the street to avoid going near the entrance.

"The number of opposed church members grew rapidly until the pastor's side was vastly outnumbered. Tensions grew so high that finally, the pastor decided to leave the church and relocate his street ministry to another location. I am afraid that the parting was somewhat bitter. And the church building and grounds are in a sorry state. That is what we have gathered to discuss tonight. We are in Brother Milan and Sister Anka's home because our beloved church is trashed. Where do we go from here?"

A tense silence filled the room. Then many people began to speak all at once—most of them grumbling.

"I told you this would happen, didn't I?"

"This isn't my problem. I didn't trash our church."

"I'm not setting foot in there until every trace of those bums is washed away with bleach!"

Inspired by vivid memories of a time in his life when disorder, depression, and antisocial behavior had the upper hand, Milan got to his feet and held his hands out for silence. A gradual hush fell on the room.

"Please stop," he implored. "We are not behaving like the followers of Christ should behave. First of all, even though things did not work out, the young pastor's plan came from a good motive. He meant well, even though he was unable to accomplish his mission. Secondly, I suspect that his impulse toward outreach has been felt in many of our hearts. I know I have felt it before. How many times have I passed by a drunk in the gutter and helped him make his way back home? Each time, I wished there was a way I could continue to help him and show him a better way to live. Finally, what does it help to say 'I told you so' now? What's done is done. All we can do is work together to restore our church."

"That's easy to say but not so easy to do," quipped a skeptical church member. "Who has the time to commit to such an undertaking? There's a lot to be done before we can worship there again."

"I have the time," said Milan.

"As do I," said the elder who had recounted the story.

"Me too," added Anka.

No one else volunteered, and to break the awkward silence, Milan offered a prayer to God for help in restoring the church. And with that, the meeting broke up, and the church members left for their homes.

Early the next morning, Milan and the elder met at the church. There was a lot to be done, but both had a lifetime of hard work experience to fall back on. They got right to it. First, everything had to be cleaned. Milan picked up all the trash, and the elder wheeled it out to the dumpster. With brooms and mops, they swept and washed the entire area. The bathrooms and showers were filthy, but they plugged their noses and sanitized everything. Then they repaired everything that had been broken—doors, windows, and even entire walls. Finally, they spent an entire week painting the church with a fresh white coat. Through it all, Anka prepared food and brought them fresh water so they wouldn't lose their strength.

When they finished, the strangest thing happened. Instead of being tired out by all the work, Milan and the elder were energized to do more. And their hard work attracted many of the church members who initially hesitated to help, and about a dozen joined the effort. With all the additional help, they were able to not only restore but also completely renovate the church. The roof and bathroom floors were retiled, a new heating system was installed, and the leaky plumbing was fixed. What started as a mere cleanup job had turned into a full-scale renovation. The church members were overjoyed. A special worship service was held to celebrate the restored church building. Milan insisted that the young pastor who left be invited. It wasn't an easy reunion, but the believers put aside their differences and embraced one another. The fellowship that they had together was truly blessed as all gathered in the house of God to worship and share His blessings.

* * * * *

Even though Milan never held any lofty church leadership positions, he frequently led his church community through humble service and a positive, proactive attitude. When something needed fixing, he was always ready to devote his time and energy to it. When conflicts arose, he was always willing to listen to both sides and mediate a peaceful solution. Leading by serving others and setting an example is often the most effective.

Even in his old age, Milan was able to have a powerful impact by refusing to get caught up in factious squabbles and by choosing instead to focus his energy on restoring the church. As a result, the church was renovated beyond any of the church members' dreams, and a reconciliation with the young pastor was effected. Truly, God works best through us when we strive to be conduits of His restorative love!

A deep respect for the ministry

"Good afternoon, sister Marta. How are you today?"

"Milan, how nice to see you. I am well, thank you. And what about you?"

The two friends chatted for a while on the sidewalk as they usually did when they happened to meet. Milan took out a *Signs of the Times* magazine from his satchel and presented it to the lady, who gratefully accepted it. In his old age, Milan hadn't slowed down in witnessing for God. Wherever he went on his many errands around town, whether buying supplies for Anka or visiting ailing church members, he carried his satchel full of Christian materials in case he had the chance to witness. And once again, the Holy Spirit opened another door for him to let Christ's light shine on someone's life.

Just then, a priest walked by. He and Marta recognized each other, and he stopped to join the conversation. After Marta introduced them to each other, Milan spoke to the priest.

"It is an honor to meet you, Father," he said respectfully. "Marta has told me many good things about you and your preaching."

"Both Marta and you are very kind," beamed the priest. "But I must say, it is surprising to hear such positive words from someone who does not belong to the mother church. These days it is more customary to hear people disparaging the clergy."

"You won't hear such talk from me," Milan assured him. "Though I may not belong to the same church as you, I, too, am a believer. And I spend time every day reading God's Word. It was there that I discovered that priests are called angels."

"Really? Where did you read that? I've read the Bible from cover to cover, but I don't remember ever having read that verse before."

"Here, let me show you."

And right there on the street, Milan took his well-read Bible out of the satchel.

"It's right here, in Malachi 2:7: 'For the lips of the priest shall keep knowledge, and they shall seek the law at his mouth: because he is the angel of the Lord of hosts' " (RHE).

"That is amazing," marveled the priest. "Truly, you know the Word of God exceptionally well."

Milan bowed his head in humble acknowledgment.

"It is what has sustained my family and me through a lifetime of trials and tribulations. Without the Word, where would we be?"

"Indeed, brother Milan. Well said."

The priest embraced Milan, and they spent the rest of that afternoon in a friendly discussion of the truths contained in the Bible.

* * * * *

As the brief story of his encounter with the priest illustrates, Milan had a deep and abiding respect for the those in ministry, regardless of what denomination or church they belonged to. Though he never had the chance to formally study Scripture, Milan always held those who did in the highest regard. This attitude was reflected in the life paths of two of his sons. The eldest and the youngest both chose to dedicate their lives to full-time ministry in service to the God who had changed their father's life and blessed their family repeatedly. And both sons not only completed their secondary studies but went on to study overseas and achieve the highest levels of academic success: they were both awarded doctorates in theology from an Adventist university.

And God's blessings continued to multiply. Just as his sons had been influenced by his faith and respect for the ministry, now Milan himself was influenced by their success. One of them brought their father all the way to the United States, where Milan had the wonderful chance to see just how pervasive the power of God was by witnessing the global reach of the church. There, he not only saw his son receive the highest academic degree but also met believers from all over the world. One of his sons also wrote a book, a companion to the Bible Study Guide that was read by millions of believers all over the globe. The grateful son dedicated this book to Milan and Anka. Milan also traveled to Egypt, where he preached at a local church. He preached in Bosnian, his son translated Milan's words into English, and the local pastor translated the son's words into Arabic. At the end of the sermon, Milan was so moved by an elder's poverty that he gave the man his own shoes. This once-in-a-lifetime trip also included a stop in the Holy Land to see the places where the patriarchs, the prophets, the kings, the disciples, the apostles, and, ultimately, the Messiah had lived and ministered. It was a profound spiritual experience for Milan and a fitting culmination of a life of faith in God.

A city of two tales

The bus wound along the road, curving by the coast of the Mediterranean. The sun beat down brightly, causing the waves to sparkle and the rocks of the countryside to bake in the heat. Milan stared out of a side window, taking in the breathtaking scenery. On his lap sat his grandchild, and nearby were Milan's son Stefan and his wife. They all happily munched on dates as they made their way up the seaside of the Holy Land.

A city by the sea came into view. As the bus drew nearer to the picturesque harbor, Stefan leaned over and spoke.

"Look, Father, at the city that is up ahead. That is Jaffa, or Joppa from the Bible. When I was little, and we still lived all together in Derventa, you used to preach sermons to us about that town. Do you remember?"

"Yes, I do," said Milan. "My two favorite stories from the Bible are tied to that town. But when I was preaching about them, I never imagined that someday I would have the privilege of seeing Joppa with my own eyes. Thank you, my son, for bringing me here."

"The thanks belong to God," Stefan responded. "If it were not for Him, none of this would be possible."

"Grandpa," said the little boy in Milan's lap, his mouth full of dates, "what stories are you talking about? What happened in this town?"

"Well," began Milan, "the first story is about a prophet named Jonah. God gave Jonah a unique mission. Most of the prophets had only the worst things to say to the oppressors of God's people. The messages for them were usually full of doom and vengeance. But God spoke to Jonah and told him to go preach to the Assyrians who lived in Nineveh. They were some of the cruelest conquerors in history. But God wanted to show them His love and grace—if they would choose to heed Jonah's message and repent.

"Jonah couldn't handle this mission. Instead of following God's instructions, he got on a boat, right here in Joppa, and sailed in the opposite direction from Nineveh. This didn't work out too well for him, and God stopped him by using a storm and a whale. Afterward, Jonah repented and carried out the mission God had given him.

"I liked to preach about this story because I could see myself in Jonah. I, too, hesitated to preach God's Word to those who opposed His people. I am most comfortable preaching in church and talking about God with fellow believers. But God wants us to step out of our comfort zones and take His gospel to those who need it most—to the unbelievers, the present-day 'Assyrians'—even though they might revile or persecute us."

"And you have done more than preach about this approach,"

interjected Stefan. "Throughout your life, you have followed God's instruction to Jonah. I can remember when you would witness to the coworkers who mocked you and to the townspeople who persecuted us. As powerful as your sermons were, Father, your example was even more so."

"It was all possible thanks to the power of God. Without Him, I could have accomplished nothing," Milan said.

"What's the other story that happened in this town?" the grandchild asked.

"The story of Cornelius. It started with the apostle Peter, who had a vision while he was staying right here in the town of Joppa. God showed him that all people are His children and that everyone deserves a chance to believe and accept Christ's love. Up to that point, many early Christians viewed the Romans as unclean people and would have nothing to do with them. But God instructed Peter to go and minister to Cornelius, who was not only a Roman but also a centurion in charge of a group of occupying soldiers. Unlike Jonah, Peter immediately followed God's command. And when he met Cornelius, Peter found that this Roman centurion had already been regularly praying, fasting, and giving money to the poor. After spending some time with them, Peter baptized Cornelius and his entire household. And so, the gospel began to spread from God's chosen people, the Israelites, to all the nations of the world."

"Praise the Lord," Stefan said.

"Yes," Milan agreed. "Just like the story of Jonah, the story of Cornelius challenges us to share the good news with everyone. Instead of focusing on the negative aspects of those who are not in our church, we should focus on their positive aspects and reach out to them with Christ's love. Who knows, we may find that they are receptive to God's grace like the Assyrians were when Jonah finally delivered God's message, or we might find that they are already keeping many of God's commands in their own way, like Cornelius was when Peter came to him."

The bus passed by the city, and the happy little group inside kept talking and reminiscing about earlier days and how God's grace had led them to this blessed moment when they could travel through Bible lands and talk about personal and present-day applications of Bible stories.

* * * * *

Milan's emphasis on sharing God's message with those outside of the faith was one of the hallmarks of his faith. Time and again, he would exhort his fellow believers to open themselves to the possibility of reaching out to those who seemed unreachable. The Holy Spirit's influence is all-powerful, Milan would argue, so who are we to deny Him the conduit of our witnessing?

If God could speak through Jonah to the Assyrians and through Peter to the Romans, He can surely speak to the people of the world through us today. This was Milan's fervent hope and prayer, and he did his utmost to follow the examples given in the Bible and to witness to those most in need of God's salvation.

God is with us everywhere

In a room darkened by tightly closed curtains, Milan lay in his bed. His cheeks were sunken, and his skin was pale. Though he wasn't asleep, his eyes were shut, and his breathing was more like panting. A light knock on the door announced the nurse, who was showed in by Anka. The nurse came over to his bedside and took Milan's hand. He sighed deeply but didn't open his eyes.

"Hello, Milan. How are you doing today? Are you in pain?"

"Yes," Milan answered through clenched teeth.

"Here, let me get something to help you with that."

"No," Milan waved her away from the morphine. "It is not the pain of the cancer that bothers me the most."

"What is it, then?" asked the nurse.

"Today is my Sabbath. I wish I could go to church to worship God as I have ever since I accepted Christ as my personal Savior. But I cannot go because of this sickness. For three months now, I have not been able to worship God with my church family. This is what causes me great pain."

The nurse took his frail hand into hers. "Dear Milan, don't you know that God is everywhere? If He is in our hearts, we can worship Him wherever we are."

In the silence that followed, a single tear trickled down Milan's worn face. When he had composed himself, he spoke, "Yes, sister, you are right. Thank you for reminding me of this great truth. Would you please pray with me?"

And, asking Anka to join them, they bowed their heads in prayer to the God who is always with us wherever we may be.

* * * * *

It was not long after that experience with the nurse that Milan passed away to sleep in Jesus and await His second coming. His battle with cancer was painful, and throughout his fight, Milan's children took turns visiting him and sitting at his bedside. One by one, they came from all over the world to comfort their father in his hour of need. They would sing and pray and recite Bible verses to him. His favorite passage was from Psalm 116. It begins with a proclamation of thanks to God,

I love the Lord, for he heard my voice;
he heard my cry for mercy.
Because he turned his ear to me,
I will call on him as long as I live (Psalm 116:1).

When Milan was in his darkest hour, struggling to cope with the horrors of the war he had survived, God saved him and turned his life around. Thanks to the healing power of the Most High, Milan found a reason to live and was able to surround himself with a loving family. As a result, he lived the rest of his life in faithful service to the One who had saved him. The passage continues,

What shall I return to the LORD
  for all his goodness to me?

I will lift up the cup of salvation
  and call on the name of the LORD.
I will fulfill my vows to the LORD
  in the presence of all His people.

Precious in the sight of the LORD
  is the death of his faithful servants (Psalm 116:12–15).

Until the end of his life, Milan lived as a witness for God, testifying to everyone he met about the Lord's unfailing mercy, boundless compassion, and, most of all, transformative power. Milan's life had been profoundly changed by faith, a change that blessed Milan's family through the demonstration of God's love in his life.

Now, Milan is resting, survived by his faithful companion, Anka—who is almost one hundred years old—seven children, fifteen grandchildren, and seventeen great-grandchildren. His labors over, one day soon Milan will rise with his family members and friends to meet his Savior and dwell with God in our eternal home.